Crossing
the Bridge

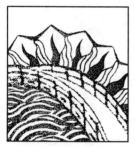

Crossing the Bridge

Creating Ceremonies for Grieving and Healing from Life's Losses

The toll for crossing to the other shore of wholeness is the relinquishment of suffering. This crossing over is what is called healing....

—Stephen Levine, *Healing into Life and Death*

Sydney Barbara Metrick

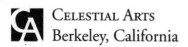

CELESTIAL ARTS
Berkeley, California

"Ithaka" from *Collected Poems,* C.P. Cavafy. Translation copyright © 1975 by Edmund Keeley and Philip Sherrard. Edited by George Savidis. Reprinted by permission of Princeton University Press.

Diagram on page 22 adapted from *The Hero with a Thousand Faces.* Copyright © 1975 by Joseph Campbell. Reprinted by permission of Princeton University Press.

Excerpt from *Four Quartets* by T.S. Eliot. Copyright © 1943 by T.S. Eliot. Reprinted by permission of Harcourt, Brace.

Excerpt from "Mental Hygiene and World Peace" by Dr. Kilton Stewart in *Mental Hygiene,* Vol. 38, No. 3. Reprinted with permission of Dr. Stewart's widow, Clara Stewart Flagg, 11657 Chenault Street, Los Angeles 90049, (310) 476-8243.

Cover design by Sarah Levin
Text design and typography by FORM FOLLOWS FUNCTION
First Celestial Arts Printing 1994

Library of Congress Cataloging-in-Publication Data
Metrick, Sydney Barbara.
    Crossing the bridge : creating ceremonies for grieving and healing from life's losses / Sydney Barbara Metrick.
       p.   cm.
    ISBN 0-89087-738-6
    1. Rites and ceremonies. 2. Loss (Psychology) — Religious aspects.
I. Title.
BL600. M48   1994
291.3'8 — dc20   94-18032
                                               CIP

Printed in the United States of America

1 2 3 4 5 6 7 8 9 10 / 98 97 96 95 94

ACKNOWLEDGMENTS

I would like to extend my deepest appreciation to the people who shared their personal stories: Renee Beck, Sondra Freundlich-Hall, Carol Ehrenberg, Malcolm Ferguson, Tobey Kaplan, Jennifer Kilpatrick, Obtumea Obtumah, Cheryl Richards, Nancy Sobanya, Todd Wagner, and Nancy Walton. Thank you to Angeles Arrien who gave me a wonderful referral, and to all the expressive therapists in R.E.A.C.H. who thoughtfully shared ideas and information. I am very grateful for the enormous knowledge and cheerful assistance of the Berkeley, Richmond, and Oakland librarians as well as those at John F. Kennedy University. Mostly, I would like to thank my editor, Sal Glynn, who created a safe and successful process for me and this book.

DEDICATION

This book is written to all of you. No one is without loss, but no one need lose hope.

TABLE OF CONTENTS

PROLOGUE

IN THE URGENCY to obtain independence that only an adolescent can know, I moved from my parents' home in the north suburbs to a shared apartment on the south side of Chicago just before my eighteenth birthday. That was my first real physical separation from my family. Eight years later I relocated to California and was only to see my family on the average of once each year. My mother dutifully called me several times a month, and my father wrote frequent letters, describing in his own inimitable style the goings on in the family, the weather, and various foods served at family gatherings. After sixteen years I grew accustomed to not "seeing" my family.

In 1988 my father began to develop serious health problems. He was hospitalized for bypass surgery, but upon his recovery he developed a series of other critical conditions. I travelled back to be with him a number of times, each time thinking it could be the last. Finally he reached a plateau and no major health issues occurred for over a year. We were all relieved but wary. Then one afternoon I received a call from one of my sisters, "Daddy died." He was seventy-eight years old.

My father's death changed my life in ways I could never have foreseen and still do not understand. I had lost people I loved before. Uncles, aunts, grandparents, neighbors, and friends had passed away and I remained the same. But my father. . . .

When I returned to Chicago for the funeral, I asked my mother for some of his things. She let me take the old photographs of me as a child from his wallet. I found the shaving brush I would watch

him use to lather his face, in my child's fascination with daddy's morning ritual. There were some coins and medals he'd saved in an old Band-Aid box that seemed to evoke memories of my childhood, too. I found photographs of him at different ages of his life, when he and my mother married, when I was a little girl, and one that depicted my father as a small child surrounded by his entire family.

I brought all these things home and set up an altar in the living room. Along with his remembrances, I placed sympathy cards, flowers, and candles. Every day I'd light a candle and speak with my father. Periodically, as I felt moved, I rearranged the items. One day I found a small cabinet-like box in the garage. I decided to make a permanent memorial to my father. It still stands in a special place in my home. I walk by my father's altar frequently, and sometimes pause to look at his face, to talk, or just remember.

Separated from my family by over 2,000 miles, the altar was my way of remaining connected with my father, just as the telephone helped me remain in touch with my mother and sisters. But I still felt isolated and alone in my bereavement. Some months later I was given a chance to do more work with my grief in the company of others sharing similar feelings of loss.

I received a call from a French woman, who described herself as a visiting anthropologist doing research for a documentary on rites of passage. Her project was to be three one-hour films exploring rituals around the world that were used for birth, adolescence, and death. We sat in my living room and discussed my work and our shared feelings about the value of ritual. Afterwards, she invited me to create ceremonies for the film series. I assembled three families with newborns to create a birth ritual, and four other adults who, like myself, had lost a father in the past year, for a death ritual.

We performed the ceremony to our fathers in the art studio of one of the group members. The French film crew set up their cameras and lights in a hum of activity while we solemnly created a sacred space by arranging a large square cloth over the floor and adorned it with ritual objects in the fashion of an altar. We entered the ceremonial space accompanied by the sounds of serene meditation music. While the music faded we each took our places, and as the final notes toned I rang deeply resounding bells. After a moment of silence, each of us in turn described the various mementos we had brought as "power objects," then lit a candle to our fathers. In a guided meditation we were directed to open ourselves to receiving a gift from our fathers' spirits. As we returned from the meditation we silently took art materials and drew images of our gift. When everyone had finished we discussed our drawings and our experience. To complete this moving ceremony, we shared a libation while a special blessing was given.

This poignant ritual helped me find further healing for my loss. The group support and sharing, receiving the symbolic gift, and having witnesses all seemed to be vital components in helping me discover the strength and beauty available in my grief. But it wasn't until a devastating fire nearly consumed the Oakland hills that I learned my greatest lessons about grief and healing.

"By mid-afternoon on Sunday, October 20, 1991, what had started as a brush fire on an Oakland hillside turned into a massive firestorm. Propelled by hot, heavy winds, the blaze raged for more than fifteen hours, destroying close to 3,000 homes and killing twenty-five people.... Within twenty-four hours a newly-formed coalition, the Bay Area Arts Relief Project recruited artists, expressive arts therapists, and psychotherapists concerned with children to volunteer in an expressive arts therapy program for children in schools affected by the fire."[1] After brief trainings, teams of artists and therapists entered the schools to help create a variety of visual, literary, and performing arts projects. As a member of the program committee, part of a team working with fifth and sixth graders, and one of the writers who documented the project, I was able to see the incredible value of creative expression and group support for those who had experienced overwhelming loss.

In documenting the project, I had interviewed many of the team members about the extraordinary work they did in the classrooms. The teams and the children created such diverse projects as building a paper box city, designing an outdoor play structure to replace the one destroyed by the fire, creating a memorial ceremony for animals lost, composing a group multi-media, three-dimensional book, and fabricating worry dolls. The stories, photographs, and projects showed how feelings of fear and sadness could change to those of hope and pride through the process of creative expression.

Working over the months with children and adults who lost their possessions, their homes, their pets, and even their neighborhoods, I saw the pain and grief, but also the love and bonding that was born from the ashes of this calamitous experience. Although grief is a very personal experience, it is one that is common to all of us. The more we create or re-create a sense of connection, the more we experience healing.

The definition of healing is finding wholeness, and we find wholeness by following principles that are timeless and universal. Whenever something is lost or destroyed, something else must be born or created in its place. This is depicted in the T'ai Chi symbol, the Taoist concept of complementarity. The opposites represented by yin and yang are in perpetual interplay. As one reaches its fullness and disintegrates, the seed of the other is born. Keeping this essential truth in mind, we can give birth to something new in our lives. By expressing our creativity we align ourselves with a profound and powerful natural process that leads to wholeness.

Being and non-being create each other
Difficult and easy support each other.
Long and short define each other.
High and low depend on each other.
Before and after follow each other.
                    —Lao tzu, *Tao Te Ching*[2]

INTRODUCTION

What we call the beginning is often the end.
And to make an end is to make a beginning.
The end is where we start from.

—T.S. Eliot, *Four Quartets*

GRIEF BEGINS IN the losses of childhood, when all we can do is ache or lament. As we continue through life and experience many other types of loss, our responses range from devastation and powerlessness through depression and anger. We think of death as the ultimate loss, but all losses are deaths. Is death really an ending—coming to the end of a linear line? Or is it, as in the cycles of nature, a stage in the process of transformation? A loss is a transition, a rite of passage, and usually a loss is painful. Whether it is anticipated or shocking, recovering from a loss is a task that is often overwhelming and frequently immobilizing.

Western culture abounds with taboos about anything painful, particularly death. Most people cannot face, much less manage, saying good-bye. With little cultural acknowledgment of certain types of loss, many passages go unmarked. Without traditions to offer guidance, recovery can be slow and difficult. We are not supposed to publicly display or reveal our feelings. Men, more than women, are conditioned from childhood to remain in control. Fear and pain make us feel vulnerable and powerless. We cannot control the elements of our lives, and that can be terrifying. When we suffer a major loss there is a reflection of our own mortality.

All losses have certain things in common. A part of your life is no longer there in the same way. You can lose a dream, an opportunity, or your loss may be something tangible—your home, a loved one, your pet, or a health problem that ends in physical loss. In every case you will be gracelessly hurled into a rite of passage. Your passage will take you into the past, the present, and the future. In the journey towards recovery you must let go of what is gone, discover what remains, and determine who and how you will be in the future.

When this passage first presents itself and you are hit with the reality of an ending, you may experience a kind of numbness. This is shock. It is too much to comprehend, too much to process. People will try to offer you support by asking, "Is there something I can do? Please let me know how I can help." For a friend or relative to be there for you is the most valuable assistance one can initially give. Once the feelings of helplessness, anger, despair, guilt, and abandonment begin their onslaught, you must find a way to contain, acknowledge, and transform these feelings.

This is where ritual can provide not only a means for processing grief in its many forms, but also a supportive structure that can bring comfort and healing. Loss hurts. Denying the pain or running from it does not make it go away. It will lie waiting to surge forth at unexpected and often inappropriate times. In this book you will find tools for transforming your grief. Learning these tools will take courage, but it will also bring you courage as you discover more of your own inner strength and power. As a human being you have limitless creative potential. Tapping into this source lets you channel the primordial essence of renewal which is echoed in the cycles of the seasons, the ebb and flow of the tides, and the restorative capacity of your own body. While you express your creativity through ritual and ceremony you can find ease through real and symbolic ways to express your feelings.

Throughout history people of all cultures have used ritual at times of transition. "Rituals carry cultural meaning passed on through the different experiences of generations, as well as allowing opportunity to create new (standards) and new metaphors."[1] In the special time and space set aside for the performance of a ceremony, an opening is created through which you connect with something greater than yourself. This connection with the sacred will allay fear and provide hope. Ritual is the vehicle with which you can safely undergo a passage.

A rite of passage includes three stages. The first is *separation.* In this stage you intentionally leave or are forced to leave some person, place, or thing that has held meaning for you. In the second stage of *transition,* the old position is no longer held but a new one is not yet present. You are in an ambiguous situation. The rituals you do in this stage are meant to provide a safe journey through this area, and to prepare you for a new position and new relationships. The final stage is that of *incorporation,* when enough of a transformation has occurred that you have a new sense of self.

In real time this passage may take a week, a month, a year, or more. This will depend on the type and severity of your loss, who you are as an individual, and what resources you have available to aid you with your grief. The ritual you create may be something that can be done in an hour or two—a single ceremony. It may be something you wish to do each day along the lines of prayer or meditation. It may also be an ongoing process that supports you throughout the term of your grief.

As a process, ritual can provide a structure to assist you through your passage. The planning, preparation, and performance of the ritual each give you a specific way to address your emotions. The ritual process becomes a "container" within which you can embrace your experience—to integrate your loss and the change it has initiated in your life and in your idea of yourself.

Even after the ritual and the change has been integrated, your transition may not be over. Anniversaries of events, new losses, or other triggers can awaken feelings you may have thought were resolved. This is normal. Integration happens on different levels over time. Once you have the tools for healing, you can use them whenever you have need. The purpose of this book is to provide you with these tools, in the hope that your journey through loss can be eased, honored, and understood.

The word ritual *comes from the Sanskrit* rita, *which refers to both art and order. Like all real art, ritual provides organic order, a pattern of dynamic expression. . . .*

—Jean Houston, *The Search for the Beloved*

CHAPTER I

The Spectrum of Loss

*There is an appointed time for everything, and a time for
every affair under the heavens.... A time to seek, and a
time to lose; a time to keep, and a time to cast away.*

—Ecclesiastes, 3:1–6

WHAT IS LOSS?

Loss is physical. It can be felt as an aching in the heart, a yawning emptiness, and a lead weight that hampers each movement.

Loss is emotional. It is unyielding grief, waves of tears, and violent undirected anger.

Loss is mental. Your mind can be overtaken by self defeating thoughts and a lack of direction.

Loss is spiritual. You question the meaning of life, the existence of spirit, and your own purpose.

Yet it is through loss that we gain new meanings in life. By embracing loss we can align with the rhythms and cycles of our selves, our living, and our world. Leaving the security and comfort of the

womb predicates birth. Many plants have seed coats so thick they must be burned to be able to germinate, making forest fires a necessary part of nature. The loss of innocence is essential to the perpetuation of the species. Loss implies change. It does not only demand deprivation, but is integral to the growth embedded in the cycles of nature. All cycles include a middle and a beginning as well as an end, and unfold in a characteristic manner. "As soon as a particular moment is identified as being part of a cycle, it becomes inextricably related to both the beginning and the end of the cycle."[1] You might say loss is inherent in life.

In contradiction to nature, we live our lives in a linear fashion. We create "probable futures" for ourselves and move through our days directed towards what we hope, desire, and expect the future to be. Imagine for a moment that life is a maze, an intricate network of winding passages with one or more blind alleys. You are traveling along a particular path that you've become familiar with. Either consciously or unconsciously you've created images about what lies ahead. If the path is pleasurable or important, you may reflect upon those images from time to time, interacting and refining them. If you know you are within a maze, you are prepared to meet an obstacle sooner or later, but suddenly—OH NO!—there is a deep chasm right where your next footfall would be. Your foot hovers in mid-air momentarily before you scramble for solid ground. Once you do have both feet back on the path, you are in a state of shock. Your heart is pounding as you strive to control your breathing. When the adrenaline subsides you may be exhausted although a level of panic might remain. What happened? How could this happen? What are you supposed to do now?

You must take some time to regain your composure and then resume your journey. But how do you do that? Is your destination going to be the same or must you change it? Do you go back to where the choices originally presented themselves and choose again? Do you even want to begin again?

This scenario may seem very real to you if you've experienced a profound loss. Grief is not only a response to the removal of a probable future, but the reaction to the withdrawal of something you've identified with. Even if it was a dream or a possibility, it was your dream or possibility and now it's gone. You have been deprived of something that you thought would be part of your future. What remains is sorrow.

Healing occurs not in the tiny thoughts of who we think we are and what we know, but in the vast undefinable spaciousness of being— of what we essentially are—not whom we imagined we shall become.
—Stephen Levine, *Healing into Life and Death*

There are many types of loss. If I ask the question, "who are you?" and direct you to take five to ten minutes to answer, including everything in the past, present, and future that describes you, you might answer like I would: "I am Sydney. I am a woman, an author, a teacher, a counselor, a sister, a daughter, a niece, an aunt. I am an artist, a seeker, a student, a city dweller, a cat owner. I am a book reader, a movie watcher, a radio listener. I am a collector, a generator of ideas."

What I've listed is only a small part of what identifies me. I am also identified by my age, my ethnicity, my beliefs, the clothes and jewelry I wear, the car I drive, and my possessions. The more things I can come up with, the larger my universe. Once these things have acquired a sense of permanence in my mind they become things in which I find reflections of myself. "There is an intimate relationship between object permanence and a sense of self-permanence...."[2] I can lose any one of these things, for any number of reasons at any time. If and when I do experience a loss there will be a void in my universe, a void that will require change in how I identify myself. The way this will affect me will depend on a number of things:

- If the loss is sudden or anticipated

- The strength of my attachment to what is lost

- My way of responding to life's challenges

- The amount and types of support available to me

- Other stressful things that are occurring in my life at the same time

- Unresolved feelings about previously experienced losses

- My feelings about my own mortality

THE MAGNITUDE OF IMPACT

Sudden loss—anticipated loss

You may look forward to some *anticipated* losses. (The projects in italic are elaborated on in Chapter Seven.) These endings include:

- graduation
  make a memory book

- moving
  take a nostalgic trip

- completion of a large project
  light a candle

@ retirement
   have a going away party with Polaroid photos inscribed by those who take them

Our society has certain ways to recognize the celebratory side of these endings. Stationery shops commonly carry greeting cards to congratulate or acknowledge the previous transitions. School graduations are particularly celebrated as beginnings and are alternatively described as commencements or promotions. In the case of graduation it is not unusual to find some behaviors that speak to the element of loss. Grade school and secondary school students sign autographs in special books or in year books along with reminders to remember certain events that contributed to emotional bonding among friends. For the most part, these anticipated endings are minimized as attention is directed to the future. The bittersweet feelings that surround the loss of the familiar and the involvement with that experience are largely overlooked. If these feelings are addressed, the memories of those times can be safely kept. Then the impending future can rest firmly on the strength of a meaningful past.

Some losses, though *anticipated* are linked with anxiety and pain. Examples of these include:

@ surgeries
   write a song

@ terminal or degenerative illnesses
   plan a memorial

@ menopause, balding, or other signs of aging
   write a letter to what has been lost

@ relationship break-ups
   burn symbols of painful memories

@ children leaving home
  make a photo collage

@ a friend moving away
  stitch a memory quilt

@ getting laid-off from your job
  keep a journal

There are few, if any, standard supports to assist people in these demanding transitions. Because these endings are not specifically acknowledged, we have a tendency to downplay or deny our feelings of disorganization and pain. Friends and family may offer sympathy and aid for the more difficult transitions, but only those who seek professional therapeutic or clerical assistance can be assured of really being heard and understood. We are told to be strong and get on with our lives, but this advice does not assuage the fear, pain, depression, and loneliness.

Consider aging. Middle age can be a time of increased wisdom, secure friendships, and financial stability. It is also when signs of physical degeneration are obvious. The blessings do not obscure the failings. Because we live in our bodies we strongly identify ourselves with our bodies. When illness develops, particularly if terminal or degenerative, it can also be emotionally devastating. Other losses in this category are painful, too; and they are made more so by the lack of suitable, compassionate interventions.

Some losses are *sudden*. Among the many sudden and painful endings are:

@ shattered dreams or illusions
  do a vision quest

@ broken promises
  write a poem

- other types of abandonment
  find a myth or story parallel to yours

- getting fired from your job
  craft a power object

- being evicted from your home
  build an altar

- accidents
  tell a story

- natural disaster
  say a daily prayer

- most deaths
  make a tribute

When someone discovers that their spouse has been unfaithful, their child has committed a criminal act, or they no longer have a job, their world falls apart. An earthquake or hurricane can tear many worlds to pieces in just moments. The death of a loved one can seem to stop the world. Yet in most cases, there is nothing to help those suffering from these enormously painful experiences. With no structure to rely upon for support, the impact of these losses cannot be fathomed.

Sudden losses can also be *invasive*. In this list are:

- theft
  find friends to call for hugs

- rape
  do a cleansing ceremony

- war
  meditate each day on wholeness

@ freedom
make a time line drawing

@ assault
work with your dreams

@ murder
join a support group

When someone has been victimized or experienced a severe trauma, a discomfort and embarrassment can affect those around them. Someone feeling angry, powerless, terrified, or humiliated is experiencing feelings that are taboo in our culture. It is not easy for people to talk about these things, but the feelings do not go away when they are ignored. They may never go away no matter what is done. They can be made less difficult to carry.

Strength of attachment

The more you value, identify, or invest in someone or something, the greater your sense of loss when it is gone. Whether your loss is "real" like losing a job, or only perceived, such as not being chosen for a job you felt right for, your feelings are valid. The following example further clarifies this idea: You've worked at this company for three years in the same position. When you began, you looked forward to a creative and interesting situation that would develop into a real career. As time passed you realized your supervisor had no intention of letting you use your skills and inventiveness to enhance your position, nor was it likely you would be promoted in such a small company. You found another company that was looking for someone exactly like you. To make it even more attractive, the position available paid $5,000 more per year than you were currently earning. You went in for an interview and felt it went very well.

On Friday afternoon, your current boss calls you into her office and says they are downsizing for financial reasons and your position is cut. You are quite surprised and saddened for a number of reasons, but you think maybe this is a sign. You call the other company to see if they have made a decision. The supervisor says he will call you back on Monday. When Monday comes he tells you they have chosen someone else. This news is devastating. You are completely crushed. It may feel worse to have lost what you hoped for, and it may take time for you to process and resolve your disappointment and grief.

You might feel sadness over the loss of your job for a number of reasons. Sometimes a loss is the conclusion of a cycle. This is more of a natural ending and requires time for completion and resolution.

WAYS OF RESPONDING
TO LIFE'S CHALLENGES

Give sorrow words; the grief that does not speak whispers the o'er-fraught heart and bids it break.

—William Shakespeare, *Macbeth*, Act 4, Scene 3

Traumatic experiences force you to look at yourself. Life has abruptly become uncomfortable and must be restored to a manageable state. But that task makes demands upon you that you might be reluctant to meet. When something produces anxiety, we have a tendency to distort or ignore it in order to protect ourselves from the pain. This is not something we do consciously. Defense mechanisms are built-in psychological regulators that work to protect us from feelings that may be difficult to handle. Threatening thoughts can be pushed into the unconscious where they seem to be forgotten. The feelings do not disappear, but we are given respite from them while we gather our resources.

Feelings are sometimes denied or covered up with other behaviors. The way you handle feelings will be contingent on your age, your gender, your cultural background, and your resources. Those who lack positive resources may greet challenges with procrastination or self-destructive conduct. While it is possible to mask fear and pain, eventually these feelings must be faced or they will demand attention.

Allowing feelings to surface, or bringing them forth in an attempt to acknowledge and address them, is the most productive form of response. It is not easy to do this if you have little access to your inner resources. Facing fear is the greatest obstacle in responding to life's challenges and can be the most difficult part of the process. The Senoi of Malaya teach their children that the characters in dreams, "... are good if you outface them and bend them to your will. If you run away from them or disregard them, they will plague you forever, or until you rediscover and outface them. Once they have appeared in your dreams, they are your property, and will forever remain an asset or a liability."[3]

Available support

Having someone to talk to that can listen and understand is an essential element for recovery. Although you may sometimes feel reluctant or embarrassed to seek help, sympathetic listening as well as more direct forms of support can provide the strength you need. When you lose someone or something that was important to you, part of your pain comes from the sense of being cut-off. That is why support is valuable. It helps you recognize that you are not completely disconnected. You are not alone.

The support can come from friends and family or from a group of people sharing similar experiences with whom you can find validation for your feelings. There is comfort in telling our story, solace in companionship, and strength in discovering that our feelings are universal.

Other stressors occurring simultaneously

Stress is experienced in every area of life. Some of the day-to-day problems like commuting, loud continual noise, and project deadlines become significant when they are joined by other stressful events. We live with multiple stressors: relationship with a significant other, family members, or other interpersonal problems; occupational issues; financial concerns and legal affairs; developmental stages of living; physical illness or injury. Good things can create stress, too. Sudden promotion, marriage, a new baby and many other gift-like changes still require adaptation, and can cause stress. Experiencing a number of significant stressors at once can be too much to handle. Our resource reservoirs are not limitless, and when we have too many demands we may feel completely overwhelmed and unable to respond.

Unresolved feelings about previously experienced losses

Life can be overwhelming. When you have to attend to more than you feel prepared for, you may neglect one or more of the issues demanding your care. This may be a conscious or an unconscious choice. When deep feelings are not attended to, the repercussions are like those that follow ignoring a deep physical wound. There will be a scar and perhaps a diminishing of function in the area of injury. That area may be more susceptible to future harm. Although we seldom treat our emotions with as much seriousness as we treat our bodies, they require and deserve no less consideration.

FEELINGS ABOUT MORTALITY

Nothing dies; death and birth are but a threshold crossing, back and forth, as it were, through a veil.

—Joseph Campbell, *Primitive Mythology*

The Buddha has said, "This existence of ours is as transient as autumn clouds. To watch the birth and death of beings is like looking at the movements of a dance. A lifetime is like a flash of lightning in the sky, rushing by like a torrent down a steep mountain." Buddhists, among others, believe that death is not the end. Those who have a sense of the continuity of existence do not have a fear of death. Perhaps it would be more accurate to say that philosophically, there is not a fear of death.

According to Hindu philosophy, the primary want of humans is "being;" to exist in a physical body. Physical death is the most frightening of all the endings as it forces us to consider the unknown. Those who believe in the continuity of existence can fathom life after death with far less ease than imaging the equally unknown experience of dying. Most of our involvement with living takes place in a semi-aware blur. The days of our lives go by quite quickly, although some days seem to be interminable. No matter the speed of passing, every day is filled with more thoughts, feelings, and activities than we can fully attend to and order. There is not enough time to process our days, much less do all the things that would require more processing. Then one day we turn around and we are forty, or forty-five, or fifty years old and realize that our youth is gone.

If you believe in the continuity of existence and do not fear death, you may have still have anxiety over the condition of being mortal. If so, then every loss is a symbolic death and reflects that mortality, and how little of the power of gods and goddesses we really have.

How Loss May Affect You

Teach me your mood, o patient stars;
Who climb each night the ancient sky,
Leaving on space no shade, no scars,
No trace of age, no fear to die.

—Ralph Waldo Emerson,
"Fragments on the Poet and the Poetic Gift"

WHETHER THE LOSS you experience has a profound or lesser impact, you go through certain phases of grieving. Each phase is associated with tasks that must be negotiated for the healing process to occur. There are a number of theoretical models that describe this, all of which can help you understand that what you are feeling is normal. I find the four phases Richard A. Dershimer describes in his fine book, *Counseling the Bereaved*, to be particularly fitting. The first of these phases is shock. This state is followed by a phase of acute grief where "the reality of the loss fully registers." He calls the next stage, straightening up the mess. Finally comes reinvesting and reengaging in life.

To clarify this process, I will weave these phases into the story of a real couple. Savannah and Anthony, a couple in their early thirties, suffered a miscarriage of what they hoped to be their first child in May, 1991. A year later, Savannah discovered she was pregnant again. Both were excited, yet concerned. Slight bleeding at eight and a half weeks prompted Savannah to see her doctor for an ultrasound test. Although the test showed normal, Savannah still did not feel relieved. Low in progesterone, she was given a supplement of the hormone for the first trimester. Despite this treatment she was still fearful, especially because she wasn't getting any bigger.

One evening she went to the bathroom and saw blood. She bled all night. The next morning she decided to return to the hospital. She flicked on the light going to her room to get dressed. The bulb blew out. "It's over!" flashed across her mind. Trying to suppress this ominous thought, she rode with her brother to the hospital where the doctors performed a second ultrasound. The film showed the baby small, but alive. The doctor sent Savannah back home. Shortly after she settled in, she began to have cramps that grew increasingly worse as the day went on. By evening she was rushed back to the hospital in intense pain. Finally, after an epidural was administered and the pain subsided, she realized that she was in labor. At 10 PM a baby girl was delivered stillborn.

The next day there was a sign on the door to Savannah's hospital room that read, "HEAL" (Help Educate After Loss). This was an indicator for the hospital social worker to provide brief counseling. Savannah was struck by the inadvertent label it placed on her—she was again faced with the task of emotional and physical healing. All the other rooms on the wing held new mothers and their wailing infants. Savannah felt cheated. That morning she left the hospital feeling empty. Savannah was experiencing the confused, dazed feelings of shock.

On the previous Friday before there was any sign of a miscarriage, Savannah had constructed an altar lined with black lace cloth. It held the ultrasound, her positive pregnancy test, and symbols of pregnancy and fertility that were deeply meaningful to her. On Monday she felt drawn to using the altar and was struck by the fact that she had unwittingly prepared a symbolic means of grappling with the loss. She arranged the sympathy cards people sent, a fragile porcelain antique baby doll, and a prayer book open to a prayer that seemed to speak to both Anthony and Savannah. They burned candles at the altar for seven days and nights. One of the hardest parts for Savannah was waking each morning and remembering the loss all over again; the intense grief, anger over the unfairness of the event, and fear that with such a lack of order more bad things were bound to happen. These fears gained momentum. She found herself having fearful fantasies that Anthony could be hurt or killed. This was the phase of acute grief. Savannah felt enraged that this terrible experience had come and disrupted her life a second time. She knew what she was in for. After the first miscarriage she felt as if she'd been held underwater for a long time and had come up gasping. This time she felt she might not come up at all. It was difficult to get out of bed in the morning. She didn't care about anything. She cried a lot. Nothing had any color.

Gradually Savannah and Anthony began the phase of straightening up the mess. They kept their altar and worked with its symbols over three or four months. In late September, they joined a miscarriage group of three other couples and a group facilitator. Savannah and Anthony brought the idea of the altar to the group and stressed how valuable a tool it had been and continued to be.

More opportunity for healing came when three weeks after the miscarriage, the hospital called requesting a decision about the baby's body. Due to a bureaucratic oversight, no one had asked them before leaving the hospital what they wanted done with the remains. After deciding on cremation, they created a letting go ritual with the baby's ashes, throwing them out to the sea in a special ceremony.

Savannah and Anthony were able to begin reinvesting and reengaging in life. Over the months that followed the grief ebbed and flowed. Sometimes it felt that healing was possible, other times that sorrow lay waiting right beneath the surface. Ten months later they felt they could live their lives again. They decided to move to California, Anthony's birth place. In one last informal ceremony they revisited the spot where they had released the baby's ashes, assuring her spirit that they were not leaving her and that she would always be with them. This was a way for Savannah and Anthony to symbolically bring closure to their mourning process before moving away.

Even when life begins again, it is not the same. After a major loss, you may find you have no reserves to deal with the small upheavals life presents. This state can be short lived or persist. It's also possible for it to return at the slightest trigger. Those who survive serious loss may experience what is called post-traumatic stress syndrome. This means continuing to re-experience the event in memories, dreams, or flashbacks. There can be emotional numbness and/or hyper-alertness in readiness for some unknown disaster. Fears can arise about things that are entirely unrelated. Sleep may be disturbed and feelings of guilt become dominant. It is not uncommon to develop self-destructive behaviors.

Why would anyone want to hurt themselves after having experienced so much pain? We all have a sense of control over our lives, largely based on a myth of constancy. This myth is maintained by the familiarity of routines and repetitions. Loss makes us feel vulnerable—out of control. Excessive drinking (or any form of self-abuse) is a way to control or "produce" being out of control. Consequently, a kind of control is re-established. (This need for control can also be met in a healthy manner with ritual and creative expression.) If you feel guilty about your loss, those feelings may also feed on other symptoms that may arise post-loss. "Part of the process of overcoming post-traumatic stress involves mourning our 'illusion of invulnerability' and our former sense of control. . . . The process of mourning is, in fact, the process of *mastering* the loss."[1]

Loss will prompt some sort of shift in identity. You can remain in the state of acute grief—depressed, apathetic, angry—indefinitely, but it is unlikely. Loss forces you to change. Your life must be modified. During your bereavement you will be different than how you usually are. Even those who do not experience grief immediately, but rather in a delayed mode or feel absent of grief, may find other people responding as if you have changed in some way.

Certain types of loss fall into areas that are taboo, and as a result bring out peoples' discomfort. People may consider it rude or intrusive to inquire about your feelings. Most people have no skill for hearing and containing other's pain. Ironically, we have an enormous curiosity about disaster and pain. Think of the people that gather around the aftermath of an accident or watch televised broadcasts of fires, floods, shootings, and other horrendous events. Innumerable talk shows reveal the most intimate and embarrassing parts of the lives of strangers. Yet this is exactly why it is possible to view these acts. They are happening to strangers.

We all need to process the events of our lives in order to find a healthy place for our responses to them. Painful events are harder to face and correspondingly harder to process. When we have the opportunity to see something as outside or apart from us, it is safer, and less painful to deal with. Even this dissociated way of facing an experience will reflect back to our own inner experience and help us come to terms with it. This is one of the reasons art and ritual are effective healing tools. But because the distance is crucial for maintaining safety it may be impossible to remove or surmount it even if the desire is there.

You may be dissociating from your experience to some degree. With all the confusion you are feeling, having people treat you differently or as if nothing happened at all, can make your experience seem rather surreal. Just driving a car downtown during business hours requires the continuous juggling and processing of hundreds of pieces of information. When you've experienced a difficult loss, you may feel as if you are moving at a different pace than everyone and everything else. Life can take on a dream-like quality. The meanings assigned to things may suddenly seem odd or insignificant.

When your loss has been severe life may feel completely foreign and impossible to bear. Consider the Greek myth of Demeter, goddess of the seed grain who produced bountiful harvests, and her daughter Persephone, the maiden of the spring. One afternoon while Persephone was playing with companions in the fields, the dark god Hades sprang up through a chasm in the earth. He abducted Persephone and carried her back to his underworld retreat. When Demeter heard the cries of her daughter "bitter pain seized her heart, and she rent the covering upon her divine hair with her dear hands: her dark cloak she cast down from both her shoulders and sped, like the wild-bird, over firm land and yielding sea, seeking her child." For nine days she searched, not stopping to sleep, eat, or wash. When she discovered the kidnapping was sanctioned by her brother Zeus, betrayal and fury added to her grief. Disguised as an old woman beyond her childbearing years, she is taken in by the Eleusinians. When she finally reveals her identity, she commands that a great temple be built for her. There she "stayed, wasting with yearning for her ... daughter. Then she caused a most dreadful and cruel year for mankind over the all-nourishing earth:

the ground would not make the seed sprout, for rich-crowned Demeter kept it hid."[2] All growth and birth were halted for an entire year. The gods, deprived of their agricultural sacrifices, convinced Zeus to restore Persephone to her mother. Because the girl had eaten a pomegranate while underground when told to fast, she must return to the underworld for a third of every year.

While this story portrays the depths of despair and profound transformation that can follow loss, it also illustrates the continuous cycle of birth, or resurrection, from death. These same themes are found in the Greek myth of the centaur Chiron who expresses the archetype of the wounded healer. The centaurs were creatures with human heads and torsos on the bodies of horses. Chiron, unlike others of his kind, was a gifted healer, good and wise. When he was accidently struck with one of Hercules' poison arrows, he knew his wound to be incurable and the only relief would come through death. But Chiron, an immortal, was not allowed to die. A solution finally came through the plight of Prometheus, the titan who was being cruelly punished by Zeus for stealing fire and giving it to mankind. Chiron volunteered to go to Hades in place of Prometheus. In this way Chiron was allowed to die, and Prometheus was permitted to go free. Later Chiron was taken from Hades and transformed into the constellation Centaurus.

The theme of the wounded healer is symbolic of an inner wound that can only be healed when some part dies. This is much like shamanic initiation. In many cultures the shaman is the healer of his or her people. The shaman embodies art, ceremony, politics, judgement, and knowledge. Becoming a shaman is a difficult and painful process. One is called to the position which is ultimately achieved after overcoming many hardships. "Knowing intimately and personally the realm of sickness, decrepitude, dying, and death readies the shaman for his or her actual mission. The shaman has a social rather than personal reason for entering these realms of suffering . . . (as the wounded healer) he or she has effected a process of self-healing as well, and is thus an example of one who has the ability to transform self, others and nature. By dying in life, the shaman passes through the gates of fire to the realm of eternally awakened consciousness."[3]

Although this is an extreme undertaking, your loss can transform you in many ways you can appreciate. As Savannah, stated, "A loss is a gain. I think that I have more grit to me now. I'm not a girl anymore." Your loss may change you for better or worse, whatever you choose. There is tremendous potential to change for the better, to discover a sense of empowerment. As you tap into the creative fount that nourishes you, it is possible to not only heal from life's sorrows, but, like the shaman, to become transformed in the crucible of your grief.

Healing through Grief or Mourning: The Journey toward Wholeness

The breath of life moves through a deathless valley
Of mysterious motherhood
Which conceives and bears the universal seed,
The seeming of world never to end,
Breath for men to draw from as they will:
And the more they take of it, the more remains.

—Lao Tzu, *Tao Te Ching*

W E ARE ALL on a journey. Whether you believe the journey begins at birth, in the womb, or when your soul chooses the body and life into which you incarnate, none of that matters as much as the journey itself and its purpose. We begin the journey as if it were a search, and what we are seeking is our "selfs." In Jungian terms, this is called the individuation process—the process of self-realization.

This process is often mythologized as the hero's journey. You can find variations of the myth in different cultures from ancient through modern times. The hero's journey includes certain ele-

ments depicted in the following diagram adapted from *The Hero With a Thousand Faces,* by Joseph Campbell.[1]

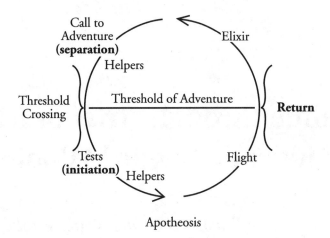

Apotheosis

Through this design Campbell describes the rite of passage having three stages: separation, initiation, and return. Your journey begins with the separation or severance from a certain way of being. You may meet this change with refusal or denial. If you do not flee from this opportunity (which is disguised as a challenge or tragedy), unexpected assistance will turn up to ease your passage. Your helper or helpers will be there as you undergo tests of grief, anger, despair, anxiety, and finally the unknown. The frontier of the unknown may seem vast and terrifying. When you face and surrender to the experience you can not only surmount it, but find it to be a region holding the gift of your undiscovered powers.

Consider the biblical story of Job as an example. "Job, an oriental chieftain, pious and upright, richly endowed in his own person and in domestic prosperity, suffers a sudden and complete reversal of fortune. He loses his property and his children; a loathsome disease afflicts his body; and sorrow oppresses his soul.... He curses the day of his birth and longs for death to bring an end to his sufferings.... In response to Job's plea that he be allowed to see God and hear from him the cause of his suffering, God answers, not by justifying his action before men, but by referring to his own omniscience and almighty power. Job is content with this. He recovers his attitude of humility and trust in God, which is deepened now and strengthened by his experience of suffering."[2] In addition, the Lord replenishes Job's prosperity in every area of his life; doubling his wealth, restoring his friends and family, and blessing him with beautiful children, and a long and happy life.

Once Job surrenders to the greater plan or greater power, he becomes a part of it. Perhaps faith is a way to transcend the fears that haunt us when we feel alone and separate. Faith in a greater power can help you return to the source. Breaking through learned limitations to unite with this power is not easy. When you experience a profound loss you may feel betrayed or abandoned by whatever your sense of Spirit is. You may feel your beliefs to be false or shattered. This is not a time to test the greater power, it is an opportunity to test your beliefs and truly understand their workings. Here is where ritual can help. During your grief, ritual can not only help you connect with something larger than yourself, it can help you actualize your experience so that it becomes a resource and a stepping stone. In this way, one cycle of the journey is completed.

Just as a man discards worn-out clothes and puts on others that are new, the embodied leaves behind worn-out bodies and enters other, new ones. Swords cannot wound him, the fire cannot burn him, water cannot dampen him nor the wind parch him. He cannot be cut or burned, not moistened nor dried. Subsisting always, everywhere, immobile, fixed is the eternal one.

—Bhagavad Gita

Before you can effectively use ritual to carry you through grief you must first understand what it is. Grief is emotional pain. Clinical psychologist Therese Rando notes, "Grief is experienced in three major ways—psychologically (through your feelings, thoughts, and attitudes), socially (through your behavior with others), and physically (through your health and bodily symptoms)."[3] Your grief will have an impact on many areas of your life in many different ways. While you are experiencing the pain you are in the process of mourning. The mourning is the journey, the filling of emptiness. Even as this happens the pain may still be a part of you.

What exactly is pain? Can you describe it? Is it an aching, anguish, or emptiness? Is it fear or futility? Is it constant or intermittent; still or in motion; sharp or dull; large or small? Where is it located? Does it have a shape? If it were expressed in color, what color would it be? If it had a sound, what would that be? Explore the intricacies of your pain. Can you make it smaller? Can you change the color, shape, and sound of it? Can you give it voice and ask it what it wants or what it has to teach? Ask it what it needs to heal and how long that might take.

If you can describe your pain, can you do it in writing? Can you draw or paint or sculpt it? Your pain is with you, yet it has probably felt like a stalking stranger. Get to know your pain. Understand it. Find out what happens when you interact with it.

Several years ago, I worked with a man who lost his memory in a motorcycle accident. He had no recall of his life before the accident. A guided meditation revealed his pain as an impenetrable brick wall. His memories were behind the wall and somehow he had to find a way for the wall to come down. Because inner obstacles are protection mechanisms of the unconscious I suggested he face the wall and try to get a sense of its function rather than attempt any radical demolition. We decided that he would carry a stool down to the end of his street to a stone wall and sit before it. He was to calm and center himself and imagine conversing with the wall.

The first day he reported feeling foolish. The wall was immovable, completely stubborn, and unwilling to respond. Still, he persisted. Each afternoon he went to the wall to talk. He found that this formidable wall was protecting him from overpowering sadness. It was not the sorrow you might think following the loss, rather the distress of knowing the kind of person he had been and the kind of life he had led prior to the accident. Because he had already changed so much, it was not difficult for him to accept how he had previously acted. As he learned to accept the old self, more and more memories returned. He was on the return phase of his passage. The more he progressed on his inner journey, the more his pain shifted and diminished.

Pain is a signal. It lets you know that something is wrong and needs attention. If your tooth hurts, you see a dentist. When you lift a heavy object and your back begins to hurt, you put the object down. It is fairly common to respond to physical pain. Yet most people address a minor physical discomfort with far greater haste than they are willing to acknowledge emotional pain. Emotional pain is "all in your mind." It is in your mind, your bodymind (the way your mind affects your body) and it is screaming to be heard. It is not your loss that will be your "call to adventure." It is your pain.

And could you keep your heart in wonder at the daily miracles in your life, your pain would not seem less wondrous than your joy.

—Kahlil Gibran, *The Prophet*

The use of creative expression or ceremony can be your "helper." When you express yourself, your "self," the core of who you are, you find parts that may be transient and much that is enduring. Grief is necessary for this very reason. You have heard the saying, "you cannot step twice into the same river." Imagine your "self" to be like the river. In some ways you are always the river. Yet, with the passing of time and all the changes that mark time, you grow and metamorphosize.

The passage of time is marked by events. The more energy something has, the more we are likely to remember it. As I work on this book I check in with friends from time to time. "I'm writing," is not much in the way of news but, "I've completed another chapter!" is. It is the marking of a challenge successfully met and mastered. Finishing a chapter is an ending but not a loss. Each chapter of a book is a stepping stone towards the next idea. Closing a chapter on an important part of your life is not the same as ending the book. The tests inherent in each chapter are the substance of the story. Meeting a challenge calls for mustering up reserves you may not know you have, or developing new resources. It also requires being with your feelings instead of suppressing them.

When your pain calls you to the journey, you may be ashamed of it. You may interpret its existence as a sign of weakness. Your pain is the guide to your strength. Even as it mandates the commencement of your journey, so it commands the completion.

If you bring forth what is within you, what you bring forth will save you. If you do not bring forth what is within you, what you do not bring forth will destroy you.

—Jesus, Gospel of Thomas, *Gnostic Gospels*

According to Campbell, at some point in your journey you reach the apotheosis—being raised to the status of a god or goddess. The point is reached where you recognize the continuity of your "self" and that your life will continue even though something meaningful is no longer actively with you. When this happens you feel you can go on with your life. You are on the return leg of your journey and may be aware of having the elixir, the magical element that brings healing. There is no predesignated time frame for the different stages of your journey. Arrival at this stage may come very quickly, enabling you to make what could be a long return comforted by reliable support.

Not long ago, I attended the funeral of man who died of a drug overdose following a deep depression. Although the widow knew of her husband's condition, his death had been an enormous shock to her. Without thinking, she allowed her daughter to take her to an Alcoholics Anonymous meeting on the day after his death. There, with a group of strange women, she shared the horror and pain of her experience. The group responded with such a profusion of understanding and support that it took her a while to be able to receive it. The compassionate expression of these people helped her realize that her emptiness and confusion were not as vast as she feared. She knew that this genuine understanding and acceptance of her feelings would continue to be there for her when and if she needed it.

I'm sure it will be a long time before she is able to make her way back from the pain of this tragic loss, nonetheless, she will not be traveling alone. Loss is a universal experience. No one can share your feelings of grief, even if they have shared in the loss. Yet the empathy and acceptance from others can make it easier to go on. A large part of moving on involves taking the experience within you and putting it outside where the burden is not just yours to carry. Other people can lighten the load. A spiritual belief and practice can have the same effect. Having the means to transform your feelings into something manageable gives you an ongoing resource for healing.

CHAPTER 4

Creative Expression and Ritual

*. . . the objects of Magic are to bring the student to an aware-
ness of his own divine nature, to enable him consciously to
integrate and unite the several constituents of his own psy-
che. It is to effect psychological integration.*

—Israel Regardie, *The Philosopher's Stone*

G RIEF IS THE legacy of loss. The pain of grief is an enemy only
when you cower in its presence. To confront pain and demand a gift transforms an enemy into a teacher. There are many
ways of accomplishing this daunting task. When you reach down
into the non-verbal part of yourself that is consumed by feelings
and allow that part expression, you echo a process that has been
used by all peoples of the earth. Creative expression is a vehicle for
transformation through art.

Creativity is exploring and trusting in possibilities not yet known.
—Gretchen Delaney, movement specialist

Making art is a healing process. In the making of art you must be present with problems and open to creative solutions. Creativity isn't something you learn or plan; it just is. This vital force flowing through and from each of us is conveyed as humor, language, movement, affection, procreation, and play. The activity of play is generally relegated to the world of the child, but it is the child within you that is the player. The inner child is associated with possibility and renewal. Both children and the child aspect of adults are more involved in the imaginary process.

Not the artist alone, but every creative individual whatsoever owes all that is greatest in his life to fantasy. The dynamic principle of fantasy is play, a characteristic also of the child, and as such it appears inconsistent with the principle of serious work. But without this playing with fantasy no creative work has ever yet come to birth. The debt we owe to the play of the imagination is incalculable.

—C. G. Jung, *Psychological Types*

The creative process and the expressive arts help answer the questions "Who am I?" and "What am I doing?" as you travel on your journey. This happens in part from the relationship between you as art-maker and the object you create. Creative expression need not be object oriented. When you have no strong motivation to achieve a finished product, the unfolding process and the creative tension between you and the work become the healing elements.

Research has shown the arts to be beneficial in many ways. They "activate mental energy by awakening and educating the imagination, the seat of our thought processes themselves. . . . (They also) develop higher order thinking skills, including the ability to deal with complexity and ambiguity; the capacity for sound judgment; attention to purpose as much as results; and the ability to consider differing viewpoints and defer judgment."[1]

When you use creative expression to produce something of beauty which can bring you a feeling of pride and accomplishment, or allow for the translation or articulation of an inner state, some form of healing can take place. The key is imagination. The poet Wallace Stevens wrote, "We say God and the imagination are one. . . ."[2] Imagination, magician—perhaps Stevens had something. Creative imagination makes ritual into art; and performance is the other connection. What makes ritual have impact is its connection to Spirit.

ABOUT RITUAL

Ritual is the vehicle by which we honor life's passages. When you celebrate a birthday, wedding, or holiday you are using ritual. When you attend a graduation, funeral, football game, or bat mitzvah you are participating in a ceremony. Ritual is common to all of our lives. When certain occasions arise we automatically respond with a form of ceremony.

Every year toward the end of December, Christians celebrate the birth of Jesus at Christmas by decorating trees with colored lights and ornaments, and surrounding the base of the tree with gifts for friends and family. Jews celebrate a festival of lights called Chanukah to commemorate the rededication of the Temple on Mount Zion, lighting a candelabra with eight candles. Those following the old religion known as Wicca celebrate the winter solstice or Yule on December 21, the time when the seed of light is born from the longest night. All of these celebrations are fitting for the season in which light begins to grow for the new year. Each are done in prescribed ways according to the traditions of that religion. Some people know the reasons behind the traditions and feel those ways best express their beliefs. Others do not have an understanding of their ceremonies but feel comforted by tradition.

You can create new rituals according to your specific needs. When you experience loss, you need to address your feelings and the changes in your life. There may be a traditional ceremony available to assist you with this. Even if a ritual does exist it may not suit your needs. Consider the traditions and customs that address loss of any type and draw elements from those that speak to you. If you are not familiar with other observances, develop your own original ideas and practices. Designing and developing a ritual is a direct and natural procedure. Each step of the ritual process— focusing on what you want to have happen, planning and preparing for the ceremony, enacting the ritual, and evaluating and incorporating the change—lets you do something productive and healing.

To create a ritual you must first have a clear idea of your intention. What do you want to achieve? What is your goal? When you have decided on the specific outcome, let your ideas of how you can accomplish this begin to flow. After you have planned the details, start the preparation. The ceremony itself is the manifestation stage. When your ritual has been completed, incorporate the changes it introduces into your life in a way you can sustain.

Creating a ritual includes:

◉ Focusing on a goal

◉ Planning

⊚ Preparation

⊚ Manifestation

⊚ Incorporation

Determining your goal follows the stages of a rite of passage: from the past, through the present, and into the future. First you must separate from the past. Rituals designed to address this stage will help you say goodbye to what is gone or to what you are leaving behind. In them you can address the feelings of loss, anger, and abandonment that arise. You can come to terms with the object or idea of your loss being a part of your past.

Some rituals are created to help you deal with the present. In the stage of transition that you experience as the present, you will no longer be able to identify with what has been lost, and will not yet have a clear sense of yourself without that person, object, or concept. You will be in a somewhat confused or ambivalent state. Your goal with rituals for this stage will be to acknowledge your uncertainty, address your fears, and find support and containment until you are ready to shift your identity and move on.

A ritual for the future works toward helping you find a new sense of yourself and incorporating that into your life and your community. These ceremonies acknowledge the change you have undergone and support and strengthen its positive aspects. Rituals addressing the future can also give you a concept of the future you want to realize, even if you are not yet ready to do so.

You may choose to design only one ritual to help you with the most difficult aspect of your transition. You can also bring all three stages into the same ritual, have a separate ritual for each stage, or design a ritual that takes place over time. This would be along the lines of constructing an altar before which you can light a daily candle, developing a regular meditation practice, or keeping a journal.

The ritual need not be elaborate to be meaningful. Lighting a candle in front of an altar can be a moving experience because you are working within the world of symbol. The symbol is the smallest piece of the ritual and the way by which you can distinguish ritual from habit or custom. The unconscious mind, or deep self, speaks in the language of symbols as in dreams or daydreams. A symbol creates a harmonic between the symbol and your own unconscious, and the collective unconscious that holds images common to all. The act of lighting a candle can connect you with memories from your childhood, or practices you have participated in as an adult. Those connections will be made with your personal unconscious and all the associations you have to candle lighting. You will also be connecting with the meanings of fire, light, bringing light, or bringing to light that have been experienced by all peoples in all times.

A ritual is a ceremoniously performed series of acts with an implied purpose. The actions are symbolically designed to connect you with something greater and timeless. Ritual encourages change because in it you experience a kind of hypnotic trance-like state. A therapeutic trance is described by doctors, Milton Erickson and Ernest Rossi as "a period during which the limitations of one's usual frames of references and beliefs are temporarily altered so one can be receptive to other patterns of association and modes of mental functioning that are conducive to problem solving."[3] The special intent you bring to a time set aside at a particular place, with special words, sounds, smells, clothing, people, and actions takes you out of ordinary time and moves you into non-ordinary time. Your focus and involvement with each stage of creating and performing the ritual puts you into the inner place of your creative imagination. This is the fertile ground in which the seeds for what you are seeking can be planted. Every moment you spend clarifying your process makes your outcome more real. You can create a world of infinite possibilities in a compelling future.

For if a man should dream of heaven and, waking, find within his hand a flower as token that he had really been there—that then, what then?

—Thomas Wolfe

Performance is a connection between ritual and art. Drama therapy is one of the expressive arts therapies and is used much like ritual. "Around 2000 BC(E), early forms of passion plays developed in the Middle East. The central character was a god-hero whose exploits were encountered both in the natural and supernatural worlds. In playing the gods, the actor, like the priest, served a spiritual function for the community, allowing others to participate in the drama as believers, more powerful in their identification with their deity. The actor also served a ritual function of repeating a series of prescribed actions and stories to insure the community that its values and myths would remain intact."[4]

Taking on a role in a ritual, or in a dramatic presentation is also like donning a mask. When we put on a lion's mask we are suddenly able to growl fiercely as we tap into our own ferocity. "According to anthropologist Joan Halifax ... the altered state of consciousness that can be produced by the sudden reduction of the visual, auditory and olfactory fields behind a mask may allow the wearer to bring out into the open certain parts of his nature that he would never reveal socially. . . . In a ritual the magnet of a mask may be seen as acting both to draw out repressed aspects from inside the personality and to draw in transpersonal aspects from beyond the boundaries of the self."[5] A mask lets you connect with and evoke energies larger than your self, as does playing a role, as does participating in a ritual. When you connect with this larger force, which may only be the larger community, you are no longer alone in your pain.

Though the pain of a loss may not disappear, your suffering can be sufficiently diminished or transformed. Ritual lets you relieve suffering by helping you regain a feeling of control as you design and implement the ceremony, and giving you a sense of distance while your attention is focused elsewhere. Ritual can be a tremendously powerful agent for change. If it is only now entering your life as the result of a loss, then your loss has already begun to bring you something of value.

CHAPTER 5

Creating a Ceremony

The circle is cast.
We are between the worlds,
Beyond the bounds of time,
Where night and day,
Birth and death,
Joy and sorrow,
Meet as one.

—Starhawk, *Spiral Dance*

CREATIVE EXPRESSION, OR creating and performing a ritual, will safely guide you through your transition. Let's look at an example designed to help a child adapt to a difficult life change. This child's experience fits the stages of a rite of passage. While it is possible to look at all the work the parents did with the child as the planning and preparation stages of a ritual, and the ceremony in the boy's room as the ritual itself, the whole transitional experience is a ritual process.

Art and ritual were born together from a fundamental human passion to express inner life.
　　　　　　—Elinor W. Gadon, *The Once and Future Goddess*

After a year of marital strife, four-year-old Max's parents decided separation would be best. Max was anxious and fearful. (He was separated from his old way of being.) He wanted to know what would happen to him and his daily routine. His father moved to a new home with a room just for Max. Both parents helped Max choose which things he wanted to take to his father's, and which things he wanted to remain at his mother's. Then, each parent individually took Max shopping. He was allowed to choose the furniture, clothes, books, and toys for each place. His father helped him set up his new room, and his mother helped him rearrange his old room. (The old way of living was gone and the new way was still unfamiliar.) His parents painstakingly worked out a schedule for times Max would spend with each of them, as well as times he would maintain his old schedule of preschool and childcare. This was carefully discussed with him. Finally, Max was allowed to invite parents, grandparents, and anyone else of his choosing to his room in each house to show his new things and explain his situation. (Max had entered into a new status and one that would take some adjusting to over time.)

A disturbing change like this is particularly upsetting for a child as it is not possible for a four-year-old to fully understand what is happening. Keeping as much continuity as possible and having consistent loving support from family and other involved people was vital for making the transition as smooth as possible.

Adults also find it easier to survive a loss if there are others to share with and receive comfort and assistance from. This may not always be available, or it may not be enough. The impact of a loss will cause reverberations that can resound for years. Even if you experienced a traumatic loss years ago, you will carry an emotional wound that can still be painful when something activates the memories or feelings surrounding the loss. You may not even be aware of what evokes an onrush of unwelcome feelings, or be able to articulate what is occurring. Loss, past or present, may cause you to unconsciously act out your anguish. Ritual can furnish a way to act out your feelings in a conscious way as it provides you with a safe container for catharsis, a sense of direction, and a supportive process.

CREATING A RITUAL

The first step in creating a healing ritual is to get a clear sense of your *intention*. What is your goal? What would you like to experience? Will you need to work alone or have others to assist or witness? Would you like to focus on feelings or do you need to address more practical issues? Your goal should be simple and realistic. If the outcome you desire is complicated, you can work toward it in stages. Repetition is one of the elements of an empowering ritual. Once you have clarified your intention you can begin the next four steps of the ritual process. These are *planning, preparation, manifestation,* and *incorporation.*

The *planning* stage of a ritual is a time for you to get to know yourself. Think about what you need and how you might achieve it. Not everyone responds to loss in the same way, and some losses bring forth many feelings and needs. When someone you love dies, your energy might be more focused on them. You may need to say good-bye, or let them know that they are loved, or complete unfinished business. Alternately you may be overwhelmed by feelings of sadness, loneliness, or anger. As you discover what is important to you, ideas for healing should begin to come forward. During this time consider if it would be appropriate to have others participate, where you would like the ceremony to take place, how much time you will need to prepare, and how much time to allow for the ritual itself. You might also consider what type of symbols would best represent your needs.

Let's look at two cases from Cheryl Richards, coordinator of the Kids, Teens, and Loss program at Vesper Hospice in San Leandro, California. A two-and-a-half year old child's home was destroyed in the Oakland hills fire. Shortly after this devastating event the boy began acting out in day care, talking about a monster in the woods, and pinching and hitting. He had great difficulty separating from his parents. It was obvious that this child was feeling very fearful and powerless. *Intention:* He needed security and power. Whatever his monster represented needed to be confronted and conquered. *Planning:* Find ways to achieve this that would be appropriate to the capacities and understandings of a young child, and were comfortable for this particular child. Drawing and acting out angry behavior were both ideas that felt right. *Preparation:* This was done by the boy's parents, bringing him into the process at a time when everything was nearly ready. *Manifestation:* The ritual involved having the boy scribble his monster on a large sheet of paper. When it was finished he was to destroy it. He stomped up and down on the drawing shouting, "Bad monster! Bad, bad monster." When it was thoroughly trampled, he buried the remains. *Incorporation:* The boy's parents talked with the boy after the ritual and continued to monitor him to make sure no more monsters appeared.

An eleven-year-old girl who had been ill and hospitalized died, leaving two brothers nine and fourteen to deal with a profusion of difficult feelings. If she could die, they could die. Children aren't supposed to die. *Intention:* The boys needed to know that she still "existed." *Planning:* Find a way for the adults to confirm their belief that she was not completely gone. *Preparation:* They decided to get helium-filled balloons and marking pens to bring to the church funeral service. *Manifestation:* At the front door of the church, the boys distributed the balloons and markers and invited guests to inscribe wishes for their sister onto the balloons. When everyone had done this, they all released the messages into the air to find her spirit. *Incorporation:* The minister invited the children to come to the church and light a candle whenever they wanted to "talk" to their sister.

The preparation stage evolves from the planning stage. As you go through the physical, mental, and emotional aspects of preparing, you can fine tune your plans until they feel right. Preparing for a ritual includes the physical work of deciding upon the symbols to incorporate into the design, and then finding and setting up everything for the ceremony. The mental work consists of refining the details. Most challenging is the task of confronting the emotions this process will evoke. Part of the function of a ritual is to provide a safe container for your feelings. The ritual allows you to access, express, and transform difficult feelings in a way that is right for you and those around you.

The poet Rilke reminds us, "Ought they not, though, to have gone and hunted up some mourners for you? Women who will weep for money, and, if paid sufficiently, will howl through a whole night when all is still. . . . We haven't got enough observances. . . . I'd like to fling my voice out like a cloth over the broken fragments of your death. . . ." In another time ritual not only allowed but required the expression of emotion, the release of pain that ultimately tapped into the source of all pain. This is the pain whose origin comes with our birth. It is a function of being here alone. Loss is the catalyst that opens us to these ancient echoes. Opening to these feelings may feel very threatening. Yet in most cases tapping into the pain provides a healing catharsis.

The tasks of the preparation stage support emotional release.

Some years ago, I worked with a dangerously overweight woman who wanted to begin a weight loss program. *Intention:* Past attempts had always been sabotaged in their beginning days. This time she felt she had come far enough to face any obstacle. As a child Dee had been sexually abused by her father. Therapy helped her understand that she had, in a sense, lost her childhood and the innocent state in which most children live. She learned to survive her loss with the comfort of food and the sanctuary of a large body. *Planning:* Dee's ritual was a new way of eating and interacting with food. She and her doctor had spent many hours planning it together. But thorough preparation was required if she was going to succeed.

Great consideration was taken to insure that the child within who still needed protection would be completely cared for. *Preparation:* Dee bought a journal to use as a way to communicate with her inner child. She was to communicate with the little girl in the role of a wise and loving mother. Each time she had a craving for food and knew that she was not experiencing bodily hunger she went to her journal and began an entry. She would address the inner child and ask her if she was calling. Allowing the child to answer in writing, she would ask about its wants and needs at that moment. As Dee began to understand what her inner child really wanted—love, safety, and protection—she was able to give that in fantasy to her inner self. Using all her skills as a compassionate adult who was actually the mother of two children, she found that as the weeks passed her inner child seemed to be growing up. Within two months she felt ready to begin the weight loss program. *Manifestation:* Still using the journal, she was able to feel safe in the smaller body that was gradually emerging. *Incorporation:* Dee found that as the months passed the inner child began to grow up. She maintained an ongoing relationship with the growing woman even as she physically became the "shrinking woman."

For Dee, the weight loss ritual took place over a long period of time. Elements of the stages would come into play as her habits and identity shifted. Some rituals do not have a clear cut beginning and ending. In many rituals the manifestation stage is a very well defined and the sought after change is immediately perceived.

Such was the case with Charles. After five years of running a successful small business with a partner, Charles decided to put his energy into another career. He and his partner Mark met with an attorney and drew up a buy-out agreement. After the initial down payment, Mark was to pay off the remaining debt in monthly installments over fifteen months. Mark made the first nine payments in a timely fashion, then started falling behind. Charles found himself calling, then pleading, and finally threatening. What was to be completed in just over one year was dragging into three. By this time Charles was involved in another satisfying venture, but the stress of dealing with Mark was getting to him. He reached the point where he knew the ordeal had to come to a stop. After much discussion, Charles realized his peace of mind was more important than the money. *Intention:* Severing his relationship with Mark so he could get on with his life was Charles' primary goal. *Planning:* After much consideration, he decided to write Mark a letter. In it, he would clearly state his feelings, dissolve the agreement, and forgive the debt. *Preparation:* Tearing up the contract and mailing it along with the letter was the final act. *Manifestation:* This was not an easy severance for Charles. Even though he felt he'd prepared himself emotionally for the task, he found the ritual to be exceptionally draining. The "letting go" took place on many more levels than he'd expected. Yet, he reported that he felt lighter dropping the letter into the mailbox, and by the time three days had passed and he knew Mark had received the missive, he was pleasantly and curiously free from caring. *Incorporation:* Charles found himself able to focus on his life and work with increasing energy and enthusiasm once he had put the past behind.

While Charles' ritual proved very effective in enabling the outcome he sought, its power was more of a secular nature. Ceremonies that are planned with a sacred design can be more compelling. You can create a ritual that specifically focuses on bringing a sense of alignment with, or connection to, your idea of Spirit. By thoughtfully choosing symbols and symbolic acts the symbol's personal level of meaning can reverberate to its universal significance. A spiritual experience joins with something larger, where you find yourself and more than yourself.

A joining with another person, family, or community can be a unforgettable portrayal of this. The following community ritual is an example. On October 1, 1993 a twelve-year-old girl named Polly Klaas was abducted at knife point from her Petaluma home during a slumber party. Echoing the myth of Persephone and Hades, a career criminal with a history of violence entered her room while she was playing a board game with two friends and carried her off. A rescue foundation was immediately formed in response. Eight million fliers were distributed and posted. Polly's face was everywhere. After an intensive two month search Polly was found dead. Adults, and particularly children, in this small quiet community were devastated. People all over were disturbed. In the words of a friend, "Polly had been mythologized." Where could a child be safe, if not in their own home with their own parents? I designed a ritual to speak to this question.

Intention: Adults needed to know they were protecting their children as best they could. Children needed to know they could trust their parents and teachers, and also trust themselves to have access to the knowledge and abilities they had acquired. *Planning:* Find a way for parents to pass on a symbol of what they felt their most important gift or teaching had been. Acknowledge the love and support always available from parents, teachers, and counselors. Show the children the strength of a united community. *Preparation:* Each adult would come up with a teaching or resource to give their children defined in a word like, love, encouragement, listening, understanding, rules, and guidance. They would either find some sort of stone to represent this resource and make it tangible, or they would paint the word onto an ordinary stone. ***Manifestation:*** The children were to enter a large room and sit together on the floor. The adults would come in, place their stones in a large container, and form a circle around the children, all holding hands. When all had entered, the ceremony guide would ring a bell for silence and light a candle for focus. She would explain the fragility of safety, the strength of community, and the power of communication. Acknowledging the children's fears, she would also remind them of their means and capacities. Explaining the symbolism of medicine bags used to hold power objects, she would invite each child to draw a stone from the container. The stone would be a keepsake and a reminder of inner and outer resources. Later, each child would make a pouch to hold the stone along with any other symbolic objects they chose. This would be a "medicine bag." ***Incorporation:*** Students were invited to keep the communication flowing. They could keep journals of their feelings, form small empowerment groups, or check in with designated adults whenever necessary. Those who were noted to required ongoing support would be referred for psychotherapy.

> *... And you who think to seek for me*
> *Know your seeking and yearning shall avail you not*
> *Unless you know the mystery:*
> *That if that which you seek you find not within you,*
> *You will never find it without.*
> *For behold, I have been with you from the beginning*
> *And I am that which is attained at the end of desire.*
>   —Women's oral tradition

When the manifestation of a ritual includes using, making, or receiving something tangible that will be important even when the ceremony has been completed, it becomes easier to shift into the incorporation stage of the process. A formal incorporation is often neglected, perhaps thinking, the ritual has been done, it's over now. For a ritual to be effective you must evaluate the change. Do you notice a shift in feeling, thinking, or acting? Are your feelings more manageable? Do you have more energy? Is it easier to go through the day? Are you comfortable? Do you feel safe? Have your daily habits—sleeping, eating, working—normalized? Have you learned anything? How do you feel about the next days, weeks, months? Do you feel you need to do more?

C. S. Lewis tells a story that illustrates incorporation as an ongoing process. "... a burly, cheerful labouring man, carrying a hoe and a watering pot came into our churchyard, and as he pulled the gate behind him, shouted over his shoulder to two friends, 'See you later, I'm just going to visit Mum.' He meant he was going to weed and water and generally tidy up her grave.... A six-by-three foot flower-bed had become Mum. That was his symbol for her, his link with her. Caring for it was visiting her."[2] This man had originally planted flowers on his mother's grave as part of a ceremony to let him honor his mother as he said good-bye to her. As time passed he felt his relationship with his mother was not over yet. He needed to keep the love and connection they'd had alive. In time his feelings would probably change. Visiting a cemetery makes death very real. His visits to the grave would be a gradual way of making the transition to being motherless in the real world.

The stages of the ritual process are not formally delineated. One stage may be indistinguishable from the next. It is not important to concentrate on getting the process exactly right. It's more important to get your needs fulfilled. You will know if you're doing it right by how you feel. Sometimes your feelings may not be clear; it often takes awhile for things to come into focus. If your loss has been very difficult you may be looking for a dramatic change in yourself. Sometimes change is subtle. Slight shifts are fine. They may be all you can handle.

Creating a ritual can be a burden in some cases. If you are feeling overwhelmed you might want to start small. Creative expression is the same and not the same as ritual. Ceremony is a creative way of expressing needs and feelings. You can use the arts in a less formal way and still experience change and healing. Putting your energy into what might be just one element of a ceremony may be sufficient. Earlier in this chapter I discussed power objects and medicine bags. While many rituals may include the use of power objects, making or just having a power object can stand alone.

Crystals are commonly used as power objects. Many people go to rock or jewelry shops and purchase quartz, amethyst, amber, or one of a myriad crystals believed to have certain properties, with the intention of making those properties more available to them. Other types of medallions—religious symbols, insignias from organizations, images of interest or affection—also are empowering by their specialness to the wearer. The macaroni painted and strung by your five-year-old child can be the most important necklace you own. Receiving something someone has made for you or making something yourself is special. You can write or make something special to help you through your transition.

CHAPTER 6

Planning Your Ceremony

... With a stick that had been purified, and which was first offered to the six directions, he drew a line from the west to the center, and then from the east to the center, from the north to the center, from the south to the center, and then, offering the stick to the heavens, touched the center, and offering the stick to the earth, he again touched the center. In this manner the altar was made and ... it is very sacred ... this center ... is the home, the dwelling place of Wakan Tanka.

—Black Elk, *The Sacred Pipe*

LILLET WORE A cloak of mourning that made her invisible. Enveloped in its dark heavy folds she moved languidly, a silent spectre. She wandered through a shadowy world alone in her grief. In her melancholic musings she found only anguish. She walked to the ocean, seeking further refuge from the life she no longer lived. There at the edge of the world she sat, staring vacantly. The waves crashed against the rocks in a roaring rhythm. Lillet felt comforted by the sounds that seemed to strike against her. A light wind came up and grew until it enveloped her in its enormous

gusts. As the arms of the wind tried to tear her from the earth, she turned to the rocks and flattened down into a crevice. Silvery drops fell from the sky and slashes of lightning ripped the darkness. Time stopped as Lillet became one with the elements. At last, the clouds parted and the blue sky gleamed behind them. Lillet emerged, cleansed, renewed. A song was running through her head—The earth, the water, the fire, the air, returns, returns, returns, returns; the earth, the water, the fire, the air, returns, returns, returns, returns.

The four elements

The story of Lillet is a fairy tale. "As with all great art, the fairy tale's deepest meaning will be different for each person, and different for the same person at various moments in his life."[1] The symbols in this story are universal. From earth centered religions to Chinese medicine, through astrology and beyond myth, the elements have important fundamental meanings. The earth represents history, that which has passed and has become a source of stability and security. The water is associated with cleansing and renewal, but also with emotion and sensitivity. Fire can be passion, inspiration, will, and the energy to act. Air expresses the qualities of the mind, thought and communication, discrimination and clarity. Using these universal symbols in your ritual will bring the qualities they represent closer to your reach.

If the intention of your ceremony is to cleanse yourself of difficult feelings, you can use any or all of the elements to express this. Each of the elements have been used to dispose of dead bodies—the earth for interment in the ground or cave burial; the water for burial at sea; the element of fire is used for cremation; and disposal by air occurs when the body is simply left, exposed. Similarly, they can be used for purification. Written feelings can be dissolved in water, buried in earth, burned by fire, or spoken to the wind. You can be washed by water, rubbed with sand, cleansed by the fiery rays of the sun, or bathed in the smoke of healing herbs. Steam baths, saunas, mud baths, and sweat lodges all combine elements to provide cleansing.

The circle

The four elements are eloquent and powerful symbols and using them in a ceremony is a way to bring balance and wholeness. Each element is also associated with a particular direction.

- East-Air

- South-Fire

- West-Water

- North-Earth

By using all four elements you are able to create a circle. The circle is one of the most powerful symbols that can be used. Continuity, wholeness, perfection, containment, safety, and balance are among the meanings a circle holds. Creating or imagining a circle around you in your ritual makes a sacred space for yourself and your ceremony.

Creating a sacred space

There are many other significant and effective methods to create a sacred space. You can define the space by:

- marking it and separating it in some fashion

- cleaning and decorating it

- altering the lighting (using candles or lanterns)

- boiling or burning scents

- ringing bells, beating drums, shaking rattles, or playing special music

- placing the participants in a certain pattern

- using a special entry (processional)

- choosing a time when the space is otherwise not in use

When you delineate and consecrate the area where you will be doing your creative work or performing your ritual, you are enabling the change you desire. Ordinary time and space are transformed into a non-ordinary, even magical setting.

Choosing symbols or power objects

Performing a ceremony in a sacred spot, an attitude of reverence, and special symbolic acts and objects makes it a ritual. The more each element of the ceremony is invested with power, the more the ceremony can empower you. Choose the items for your ritual with care. For a letter-writing ceremony, you can use expensive, formal looking paper to make the letter feel more important. Choose paper in a color that represents your feelings. The writing can be done in a room where the desk or table has been cleared, certain objects like burning incense placed upon the writing surface, complete silence, and a brief prayer or meditation said along with the lighting of a candle. The completed letter can be placed in an envelope that matches the paper and sealed with wax. Pass the letter through the incense with a prayer that it be received in accordance with your intentions and your goal be harmoniously accomplished.

The tools or objects you select should have meaning for you. It is not important whether you buy them, find them, make them, or some combination thereof. When you craft an object it has more of you, but any object can represent your feelings if you choose it with thought.

The altar

When using symbolic objects in your ritual, you need a place to put them. While you can use the ground, and in some instances this may be fitting, it is easier to have a table or stand as a workplace. "The word 'altar' derives from the Latin *altare,* a high place.... Elevation allows you to see your surroundings.... High places also allow clearer access to viewing the heavens, to metaphorically entering other worlds or planes of consciousness, and to receiving the guiding light of Spirit...."[2] You can create an appropriate altar by covering a table with a special cloth, decorating it to your taste, and arranging your ritual objects in a manner both useful and pleasing.

Now that you have gone over the instructions for planning a ceremony, use the following questions as an exercise to help you get in touch with what will work for you.

GUIDELINES FOR PLANNING YOUR RITUAL

Intention

- Consider what has happened, how you feel, and what you need.

- Describe these things as best you can.

- What is the goal you wish to accomplish?

- How will the achievement of this affect your life?

- Is it realistic? Is it feasible?

Planning

- When do you feel you can do this?

- Can you do it all at once?

- Who, if anyone, do you wish to join you?

- How much or how little do you want them to do?

- Do you want someone else to facilitate?

- Where do you feel you could best achieve your purpose?

- What do you need to make this space right?

- What symbols or symbolic acts would you like to include?

- What kind of activity would be the most comfortable and effective for you?

Preparation

Take a few minutes to read the following lines thoroughly. When you've finished, close your eyes and take three very deep and relaxing breaths. In your imagination create a movie you can either watch or enter into and be a part of. When you finish, open your eyes and write down answers to the questions.

You see the space you have decided on. Everything is exactly right— very safe, very comfortable, just like you need.

- What did you see?

- Can you create that for your ritual?

Go back into your imagination to get more guidance.

Return to the space and let yourself become aware of any colors or images, sounds or voices, smells, feelings, or movements. Notice what is happening.

- What did you discover?

- Was there anything there you can use or need to change?

This time, when you return to your imaginary space, you can let the ideas for your ritual show themselves to you.

Find yourself there in that space doing exactly what you need to do to find the outcome you desire.

  ❧ What happened?

  ❧ Describe as many details as you can.

Take your notes and reread them. Make any additions or changes that come to you, then put them aside. In a day or two, you can read over them again. Keep doing this until you feel comfortable with what you have. When you are satisfied you can begin the physical preparations for your ceremony.

As you prepare for the ritual, unexpected feelings may arise. Acknowledge them, but do not let them turn you away from your ceremony unless you feel overwhelmed. You can always return later. Actually, this is another part of the process. If you are comfortable with your feelings, continue along as planned.

CHAPTER 7

Manifestation

Ritual requires us to really see. What we are able to see if we use our eyes without censorship and prejudgments is a virtual image. It is real, for when we are confronted by it, it really does exist, but it is not actually there. The reflection in a mirror is such a virtual image; so is a rainbow. It seems to stand on earth or in the clouds, but it is not tangible. It is the unspeakable, the ineffable made visible, made audible, made experiential.

—Jamake Highwater, *Ritual of the Wind*

Back in chapter one, I gave examples of the range of losses you might experience along with possible projects or rituals to address each kind of loss. Following are brief descriptions and instructions for these projects. Use any of these ideas to fulfill your specific requirements. Some can be adapted for use with a partner or a group. You can also combine several of the ideas or add thoughts of your own.

Make a memory book

A memory book is a scrapbook that includes photographs, cards, pieces of writing, drawings, and other remembrances. Select a distinctive notebook or journal, or bind together separate sheets and cover them with material. The book itself can be made of most anything. Take the time to think about each thing you include. As you do, attend to your feelings. Write your thoughts or feelings about different memories in the book, and include the emotions the project evokes. Keep the finished book in a special place where you can interact with it. Add to it over time if you feel inclined.

Nostalgia trip

If you're leaving someplace that's been important to you, you can take a nostalgia trip to say good-bye and mark your memories. Nostalgia trips are also good on return visits to a significant place. As you travel through the rooms, or streets of the place, let your memories—both good and painful—return to you. Mentally mark the ones you'd like to save. Take photographs to be highlighted in a frame or album. Release those memories that trouble you. Imagine all your energy evaporating from that place leaving it devoid of any traces of you. Envision golden light, like bright rays of sunshine, filling the area and leaving it ready for something new and good to happen there.

Candle lighting

Lighting a small red candle in a holder is not the same as lighting a thin black sparkler candle, or a large white candle encased in a colored or clear glass. A candle you mold from melted paraffin and inscribe with special words or symbols has a different feel. Choose or create a candle that matches your feelings and desires. Think about the color of the candle. What does that color mean to you? Use that meaning in an affirmation. "With this green candle, I bring growth and healing to me." It can also be a request: "As I light this blue candle I ask that my mind becomes as clear as a cloudless summer sky." Light the candle to draw the light of Spirit down to ignite your personal flame. Let your mind explore the properties of fire as warmth, light, illumination, awareness, and a connection with Spirit. Let the candle burn all the way down. If you must put it out, pinch the flame to preserve your intention. Blowing the flame out disperses the energy you have brought into focus.

Going away party with Polaroid photographs

If you are leaving a group and plan to have a going away party, you can add an extra touch by renting a number of cameras that provide instant photographs and buying disposable cameras. Guests can write their sentiments on the backs of the instant snapshots. When the other pictures are developed later, you will be able to look back at other people's points of view. Another way is with a video camera. You can use it to film, interview, and offer commentary.

Song writing

Words have power. Written or spoken, language has the potential to amuse, convince, anger, soothe, educate, and entertain. Music has a power of its own. Through music we can enter other worlds, both literally and figuratively. Imagine what can be done by combining words and music. Give your feelings words, rhythm, and melody. Transform your loss by expressing it as song.

Memorials

Memorials help survivors remember the life of someone who has recently died. They serve as a forum where friends and family can share cherished memories and learn more about the deceased.

Many people hold memorial services for pets, too. Even places can be memorialized. Homes, temples, or land somehow destroyed can be severely missed. Establishing and sharing memories brings the past into the future.

Several years ago, I officiated at the memorial of a young man I'll call Maurice. The ceremony was held in the lush, green yard of the home belonging to a good friend of his. Terraced gardens surrounded a leaf-veiled lawn creating a setting both peaceful and stirring. Many of his close friends were in attendance. I began the ceremony with a welcome and brief statement of intention. Not knowing the deceased, I interviewed a few of the early guests to get a sense of the man we were honoring. Their words, stated as quotes, formed my opening. After speaking briefly about his life, I read the following poem.

> *Do not stand at my grave and weep*
> *I am not there. I do not sleep.*
>
> *I am a thousand winds that blow.*
> *I am the diamond glint on snow.*
>
> *I am the sunlight on ripened grain.*
> *I am the gentle autumn rain.*
>
> *When you wake in the morning hush*
> *I am the swift, uplifting rush*
> *of quiet birds in circling flight.*
> *I am the soft starlight at night.*
>
> *Do not stand at my grave and weep.*
> *I am not there. I do not sleep.*
>
> —Anonymous

One of the mourners baked a cake to be used in the ritual. The cake, surrounded by sweetly-scented gardenias, was placed at the front of the altar. A tall white candle burned, representing the spirit of the deceased. Beside the cake sat a basket of small candles. Each of the mourners came forward and told of their personal feelings about Maurice. Some recounted a story of a time they'd shared. At the end of each statement the speaker took a candle from the basket, lit it from the large candle, and placed the burning candle in the cake. Everyone took a turn, and before long the cake was bright with the glow of many flames. Although a beloved friend had died, his spirit would live in those whose lives he'd touched. The brightness of the burning candles showed the strength of the connections that remained.

Letter writing

Even when you foresee an ending and can plan for it, you can't really predict the aftermath. Sometimes it takes a while to recognize what you feel and need to say. Our unconscious minds work in ways that may seem foolish to our conscious minds; we can talk to people or things that no longer exist, or not in our presence. Here's where letter writing is a useful practice. Whenever you have any unfinished business, write a letter stating exactly what's on your mind. Save the letter, burn it, bury it, read it to the stars or the wind, or to the image of someone who needed to hear it. Whatever you do with the letter has importance. However, the task of writing is often the most healing part of the process.

Symbol and memory burning

Fire has the ability to purify and transform. When you are using fire for this purpose you will find it to be more effective if you use a ceremonial fire. Select a spot in nature where you can focus your thoughts or do a ritual before a fireplace or outdoor grill. If you choose a place in nature find rocks to make a fire breaking circle, use a fire pit, or another safe container. Before you build the fire, focus your thoughts and center yourself. Imagine that the spirit of fire which holds the power of heat, warmth, and transmutation is alive in the flames. Ask that whatever safely burnable symbol you have chosen to release be taken by the flames. As the flames devour the symbol ask to experience release or transformation. Throw sweet herbs into the fire afterwards as a thank you gift to the spirit of the fire. Wait until the fire dies or extinguish it with earth or water. Take some of the ashes to combine with soil and use the mixture to plant the seed of something new.

Photo collage

Photographs are one of the more effective means of eliciting memories. There are several ways of using these pictures in a collage. One method concentrates on finding photographs of who, or what you wish to remember. Viewing the images taken over the years is a good way to go over the special times. Arrange the photographs in pre-made frames that hold a number of pictures in a pleasing grouping.

Another way of making a collage involves a bit more artistic expression. Choose one or more pictures. Then, thinking about what these mean to you, look for other words, cards, pieces of letters written or received, symbols, and magazine images that support your feelings. You can arrange these things on poster board or other sturdy material. Cover the board with velvet or paint, then glue the photographs and other things to it in a meaningful way.

Memory quilt

"Both quilting and embroidery, as well as other lasting arts, bridge the present, past and future and offer a way by which each generation can hand its messages to the next.... Quilts are used in communities to mark life transitions, such as celebration and loss."[1] When each member of a community contributes a square to a quilt, the finished piece becomes a lasting representation of the cohesiveness and common vision of a group. A quilt can be just as meaningful if made by only one person. Every person has many memories and many stories worth preserving.

You can make a quilt into a story by creating separate squares each depicting a particular scene and then stitching them together in the order that provides the best flow. For lifelike scenes, use a slide projector to cast an image onto a piece of cloth. Trace the image with a pencil, then embroider or paint with fabric paints. Your quilt can be one large picture or many small ones. You can add words with embroidery or fabric paint, and even stitch symbolic items or appropriate memorabilia onto the piece.

Journal work

Keeping a journal is like having a friend you can trust completely. A journal can hold your dreams, wishes, thoughts, feelings, and questions. You can write in it at a specified time each day or when you're so inclined. Journals can be all words, all pictures, or any combination of the two. Buy or make a book that will be used only as your journal. Decorate it to make it more personal, or begin it with a quotation that is bound to your intention. You might find it helpful to make your entries on only the left-hand page. The opposite page can be used for later commentary or to paste pictures or words you run across that enhance and support your thoughts.

Vision quest

A vision quest is a retreat, a journey to a secluded spot where you can withdraw from the demands of ordinary life in the world and reconnect with the pulse of nature. Take a day or two and go away to an isolated and peaceful spot or work with a guide who can provide a formal experience. Professionals provide tools to experience a deeply moving rite of passage. The journey begins with the separation. Over a period of months, you prepare to leave behind all the securities and attachments of the world. As you get close to the time of your quest you will be instructed in the specifics and made ready with ritual cleansings and diet changes. You will select a site that will become the sacred space to await your vision. The quest proper begins when you enter that spot alone. The threshold stage occurs as you discover, that you are alone with a stranger and that the stranger is you. In the course of the three to ten days, a birth occurs. Your soul is revealed to you and you must decide to embrace it. Newly born, you finally return to your group. There you can "decompress" before going back to the world. The incorporation phase of the quest is as difficult as the others. Now that you have experienced a vision or awakening, how do you live?

You might say a vision quest is a kind of self-imposed loss. The transformation that occurs will be profound. The quest will prove your resilience unequivocally.

Poetry

Some of us are natural poets. One definition of poetry refers to it as "the moment illuminated." There are many kinds of poems and not all of them rhyme. Poet Tobey Kaplan contributed this poem as one of several she had written after losing a finger in an industrial accident.

> *Making little rock piles into castles*
> *as the sun floats downstream*
> *there's something missing:*
> *the evening closes in from far away*
> *when I go out to buy wine.*
>
> *If they notice, they usually ask about my finger;*
> *and then I remember your throat*
> *I'll taste with wine*
> *no candles but little flares*

and then I hear your familiar truck
surfacing up the road dotted with pine cones
as it rumbles over sleepy hills,
grinds over the gravel into parking.

They ask me why it's missing
how did I lose my finger?
I think of cuddling under thick blankets
but they point to where my right pinky should be
the shock of dull pain
the constant loss that says "be careful, pay attention"
it woke me up and how it could've been worse.

Loss, that intense burst that inspires this love;
the fear of loosing
as other people I've lost float down streets
or shady paths, purposeful in their destination
to home or some other place
but you walk up the stairs
you know that part of my hand

and those other people, we'll just keep wondering
what they are missing.

Parallel myths

You and your story are unique. Yet there is a universal element to most stories. Finding a myth or tale that echoes yours is another way to discover that you are not alone.

I spoke with a woman who described herself as being in the throes of mid-life crisis. She felt she had changed greatly in the past two years to the point where she no longer recognized herself. But there was a discomfort with the change and a fear that she had made some wrong choices in her life. Her anxiety reached such a level one evening that help was necessary. To calm herself until morning, she picked up a library book checked out the day before. As she began to read she felt the words in the chapter were written for her:

"... these have been two of the most difficult years I have ever lived through, and I think it has been difficult for all my friends as well. In fact, there has been so much stress.... I feel right now that I am struggling every moment of the day and night just to maintain my equilibrium."

"But you're maintaining it very well," she answered. "You don't give yourself enough credit. That has always been a difficulty for you. You are very critical of yourself.... You are doing a lot in the world, and because of your childhood struggles, you still don't believe you have accomplished much. It would help you if you would relax a little, within your own heart, and accept the fact that everything is going to be okay."[2]

Reading these pages had a marked effect on the woman. She felt as if she had been brought to her senses. The appropriateness of the words coupled with the odd coincidence of finding them produced a magical solace. In this instance, finding a parallel story had added power in that there was instruction for relief and comfort given by a spiritual guide that had direct application.

Craft a power object

A power object symbolizes strength, safety, security, or mastery. Being with and using this talisman will open a door to the essence of what it represents. When you create and consecrate a symbolic object you invest it with the capacity to be a useful tool. A kind of reciprocal relationship is formed. You give power to an object and it returns power to you.

Some years ago while visiting a friend, I noticed a brass figure about two inches high sitting on a bookshelf, a Buddha sitting in perfect repose. I reached toward it and felt an enormous energy emanating from this small form. As I cradled the statue in my palm my whole body seemed to become lighter. "Can I have this?" I blurted out to my friend. "Yes, of course." he answered as casually as if I had requested a glass of water. I carried the Buddha home in my pocket and thought about where I should keep it. I found a delicate hand-stitched circle of lace to place beneath it, and a tiny silver necklace to encircle it. Clearing a shelf, I arranged these things along with a handful of small rose quartz crystals carefully set in loops of the chain. Into the center went the Buddha. I stood before it and felt an incredible sense of calm. It was as if the statue reflected this quality to me. To this day, gazing at it gives me a feeling of serenity. Although the statue sits in a very accessible spot, no one has ever touched it.

I did not make the Buddha, but I did make it into a talisman by giving it a special treatment and placement. Another approach is to take items that may have symbolic meaning and join them into something. I've found an old ivory mah jong piece that I glued meaningful things to and turned into a brooch. Found objects like shells, rocks, feathers, and wood can be glued, carved, wrapped, decorated and worn or hung on doors and windows.

To make a power object or talisman, think about what quality you would like it to embody. What symbolically represents that for you? If you don't know what symbols to use, go on a hunt. Holding the idea in your mind for a week, ask for the symbols to come to you. Notice what things you are attracted to and how you might use them. If something shows up right away, use it immediately, or wait for more things to add to your piece.

Build an altar

The setting I created for the Buddha in the previous example is one illustration of an altar. A power object can be an altar and vice versa. Altars are sacred places. They can be used for offerings to a higher power or as a place to worship. Generally a table, mantle, or shelf is used as the foundation. An ordinary piece of furniture can be transformed with a select piece of cloth or covering. Because you will use the altar as a place of focus, it should have its own site. The items you chose to adorn it with should have special meaning and support the intention the altar is created for. Using a symbol from each of the four elements, earth, water, air, and fire is appropriate as this represents balance and wholeness. Some people add fruit, flowers, or incense as offerings. Your altar or altars can be composed to last or to be changed over time. Once you have created an altar you feel comfortable with, use it in a ceremony, as a place to pray or meditate, or simply as a place to find your own center.

Construct a reliquary

A reliquary is similar to an altar and not unlike a Self box. It is a place to honor relics and mementos, particularly of someone who has died. An icon can be used as the centerpiece or in a collection of meaningful items. "People like to keep mementos of dead people they loved, and unless tabus *(sic)* have specifically prevented it, the custom has always been widespread. . . . They can be either the possessions of the dead, or a bone or hair given as a personal relic, or specially made things prepared for the occasion—mourning clothes, gloves, cards, cake (wrapped in white paper sealed with black) and jewelry."[3]

Tell a story

Your experience of loss is part of the story of your life. Carrying an untold story can be a demanding burden. When you keep your loss in the dark, its whole truth is not revealed. Taking it out into the light allows you to experience it from other more comfortable and useful perspectives. Translating your experience into a story turns it into a teaching tale. Whether you write it or verbalize it you will learn something from hearing the words.

Pray

Prayer is used for praise, thanksgiving, supplication, and transcendence. Prayer acknowledges something greater, and in so doing, connects to it. Prayer takes you out of yourself at the same time that it brings you home. You need not be religious to pray. Prayers can address a higher power, all there is, love, hope, your ancestors, and your strength. Ritual is a prayer. There is no special time or place required for prayer to be effective. You determine when and where is most appropriate for you.

Make a tribute

While I was collecting materials for this book, someone gave me a program booklet from a concert performed by the American Bach Soloists as a special tribute to a local man who was noted as a physician, athlete, and researcher. In addition to loving descriptions of the attributes of the deceased gentleman, the booklet notes, "This concert of Johann Sebastian Bach's music is meant as a living celebration of T's full and rich life and a reflection of his passion for living. To him, Bach's music represented an exultant creative expression of man's interaction with God. The music presented this afternoon was carefully chosen because of its personal importance to T and his life. Thank you for joining us in this musical celebration of a life well lived." The program named the pieces, provided texts and translations, and included a few personal anecdotes.

Another more simple and very tender recognition entitled, "A Tribute to My Ma" was written and read by a loving son at his mother's memorial service. In it he quotes Henry David Thoreau, "The death of friends and loved ones will—and should—inspire us as much as their lives. Our memories of them will be encrusted over with sublime and pleasing thoughts, not as monuments of others, which are often overgrown with moss. For our friends (and my mother) have no place in the graveyard."

Cleanse with the elements

Elemental cleansings can be very healing. A mudbath or a soak in salt water or Epson salts are good ways to release tensions using earth and water. Any kind of bath can be turned into a purification by adding herbs or oils to the water, lighting candles, playing soft music, and creating a healing environment. Laying in the sun (using sunscreen, of course) uses fire and air in a healing way. You can sit before an open fire or fireplace to cleanse yourself with fire. Incense smoke or the smoke of burning herbs is another way of using fire and air.

In addition to using the elements to provide cleansing for yourself, variations of the above options can be used to purify places and things.

Meditate

Meditation is the way to inner wisdom. There are many forms of meditation. Some use imagery; some are guided journeys led by another. An excellent example of this type is found in Ram Dass's book, *Grist for the Mill*. The most basic form of meditation is following your breath. Choose a secluded spot where you can remain uninterrupted. Sit cross legged on the floor or in a straight-backed chair with your body erect. Close your eyes and begin to attend to your breath. There is no need to change your breath in any way. Just notice the breathing in and breathing out, over and over. You will find thoughts drawing your attention. When you notice that this has happened, bring your focus back to your breath. Plan to do this for about ten minutes to start. Do it every day. Let this time of the day be your time. You deserve it.

Draw a time line

A time line drawing gives you a perspective on your life. Thinking about your loss as an event or experience that is part of a larger picture can be very helpful for understanding how the importance changes with time. To do this, draw, paint, or collage your life as a line with depictions of the things you remember or want to mark. You can make the line any shape, make yearly markers or provide dates, add pieces of paper, or fold the paper by years. Do whatever feels to be the best way to represent your life. Place your current loss experience somewhere in the middle rather than at the end, so you can work on your ideas and plans for the future. The past is not actually real. The memory of the past influences your thinking and behavior. The future is even more flexible. Be creative in designing a positive future for yourself.

Work with your dreams

Symbols are the language of your unconscious mind, or deep self. Dreams are a way your unconscious communicates with you in symbolic form. Your dreams not only reveal what is occurring within you, but are also a reflection of your inner responses to outer events. Write down whatever you recall upon waking. Record your dreams on the left-hand page of a special journal, and write your thoughts, feelings, and interpretations on the right-hand page. Discover what your dream symbols and characters are trying to tell you by mentally asking them and imagining the answers. You might also try imagining a particular person or symbol and describe yourself from that state. Look for images or photographs that remind you of a dream and paste them into your journal. Pay attention to recurring dreams or repetitive dream themes; these point to important areas of focus.

Join a support group

There are many different types of groups. Some are specifically composed of people of the same type, like teens or single men; others are mixed. Groups can have a particular focus, or be open to addressing many different issues. Groups may rely on an approach like drawing, or non-verbal techniques. Once you find a group that seems to fit your style and requirements, you have a time, place, and group of people with whom you know you can receive support and understanding.

You can always place an ad in a local paper for others who share your type of loss. It's easier to join a group that has a professional leader. An experienced professional knows how to run a group and what to offer. On the other hand, you might feel more comfortable with a completely informal group. You can use the same guidelines with a group as you would to create a rite of passage ritual. Define your intention for getting together. Plan how you would like your times together to go. Prepare for your meetings. Meet. Evaluate each session.

Make a memory jug

"... The memory jug or urn ... (was) crafted around the country in the early part of this century by women who recycled sewing scissors, keys, button hooks, combs and costume jewelry in putty, gilded with gold paint.... When executed by someone with the soul of an artist the craft transcends the merely decorative to become truly memorable and moving art."[4] A memory jug may be particularly appropriate if your loss was a death and you would like to have a genuinely meaningful urn for cremated remains. However, you can make a jug just for the piece itself, valuable by the choice of memorabilia. You can also make a container that can be filled with other things to cherish.

Construct a self box

A shadow box or miniatura—the Self box—is a way to tune in, acknowledge, and express your "Self." Using boxes of any type (cigar, shoe, flatware, or old empty drawers, decorate and fill the box to represent your inner and outer self. Get in touch with what you will assemble by using meditations, discussions, and other safe and relevant methods. Your box can hold photographs, memorabilia, found objects, made objects, and more. A finished box is a power object you can use or admire.

Do a give-away

When you do a give-away you are making a sacrifice or donation. "... giving is a sacred deed and is pleasing to the Mysterious One who gives everything."[5] When you give in someone else's name, you are paying tribute to them. Giving a sacrifice in the name of Spirit recognizes the eternal ebb and flow of life. Emptying yourself makes a place for you to receive.

Black Elk said, "giving is a sacred deed." Doing a give-away, keeping a journal, or creating an altar should all be done in a sacred manner. The ideas presented in this chapter are forms of creative expression. Creation or generation is the original act and one of enormous power. To experience empowerment you must use power responsibly—in a sacred manner.

Whether it's blood, water, sake, incense, money, prayers, dance, art, future devotions, animals, vegetables, symbols, power, emotion, or one of another endless number of possible things, both tangible and intangible, the religious sects, and magical practitioners of the world have given offerings and sacrifices to higher powers for all of human history....

—Denny Sargent, *Global Ritualism*

CHAPTER 8

Incorporation: Re-Writing the Story

I have made your sacrifice.
I have prepared a smoke for you.
My feet restore thou for me.
My legs restore thou for me.
My body restore thou for me.
My mind restore thou for me.

Restore all for me in beauty.
Make beautiful all that is before me.
Make beautiful all that is behind me.

—Navaho Night Chant

WHEN THE ANTICIPATION of a fearsome or painful event, like giving a speech or having a tooth pulled, causes dread and anxiety in your imagination, it is not unusual to find that the event itself is not as bad as imagined. The ability to create a vivid episode that you could enter into gave you a way to endure the real experience. By surviving the imaginary ordeal, proof of your resilience is gained.

While many people make up stories about the future, most deny or refuse to think about the possibility of actual disaster. Dwelling on a possible traumatic loss would be considered morbid. Nonetheless, these events do occur. Tragedy, loss, and despair are universal experiences. Yet we rarely make physical, much less emotional, preparations for any misfortunes we will encounter. When a calamity does occur we think it happens only to us. Emotionally unprepared, we feel lost, helpless, and alone.

We are alone with everything we love.

—Novalis

We are separate but not alone. There is an "eternal conflict between Eros, the myth of love, and Thanatos, the myth of death. The former draws people together, leads to friendship, interdependence, and all the constructive aspects which make for unity with our fellow men and women. . . . Thanatos, the myth of death . . . includes many phases, including illness, fatigue, and all of what Paul Tillich called non-being."[1] Loss awakens the myth of Thanatos. As you seek balance and turn towards Eros, loss can lead you to wholeness through two of the most healing gifts, connection with yourself and connection with others.

We connect with others through the universality of our experience and the support we can receive. Ritual enables the connection with ourselves by using creative expression. Ultimately, any creative act serves to connect us with something greater as well.

"Works of art are produced, great poetry is written, ideas spring up, all from the conflict of Eros and Thanatos. There is no creativity without this struggle."[2] The creative life-force must be stimulated to bring balance back into your life. Using creative expression alone will initiate the healing process. For the healing to be deeper and more meaningful, combine the arts with ceremony. Ritual is a way of physically expressing a myth or story. Art, myth, and ritual are all interwoven and inseparable. Myth is a way of telling of a creation, a sacred story of how something originally came into being. "In short, myths describe the various and sometimes dramatic breakthroughs of the sacred (or the 'supernatural') into the World."[3] Because our lives in the world are in eternal transformation, a rhythmic cycle of creation and destruction, we must also recreate or renew the world in symbolic form each year as we mimic the cycle of time ending and beginning anew. The creative force is imminent and eternal. It re-establishes and stabilizes the world. Religious scholar Mircea Eliade says that ritual replaces ordinary, linear time with the sacred Time of myth. This brings us to the primordial position of creating along with the gods and goddesses. You must begin your life anew and re-create your world. Enter into the myth and tell your updated version.

[The] revolt against the irreversibility of Time helps man [sic] to "construct reality";... assures him that he is able to abolish the past, to begin his life anew, and to re-create his World.
           —Mircea Eliade, *Myth and Reality*

In the aftermath of any disaster, people tell their stories. If the event had a large impact, the media will be present seeking emotional tellings. There will be a myriad of replays on the news, photographs of the tragedy in the newspaper and magazines, and discussions on the radio. Movies depicting and dramatizing the event may follow. Psychoanalyst Sigmund Freud theorized that the tendency to repeat painful experiences is an attempt to contrast the original experience of being a passive victim. We also do this because of our need to find meaning in the events of our lives.

The stories we tell about our experiences belong to us. We tell them from our perspective. They are colored by our feelings. These stories can be told in dramatic fashion. The feelings can be exaggerated until they are exhausted. The stories can be retold with different beginnings, middles, or endings. This is the function of ritual. "Rituals are physical expressions of the myths."[4]

Myth functions in a society as a . . . model for behavior that also explains the origins of the world, life on earth, death, and all other experiences of human existence. . . .

—Arthur C. Lehmann and James E. Myers,
Magic, Witchcraft, and Religion

The myth at the core of all healing work is the myth of death and rebirth. Your loss was a death or sacrifice. To continue onward the cycle must continue. The wheel must turn.

WRITING A HEALING STORY

- We all create stories in our heads about our past, present, and future.

- Mental rehearsal can help us successfully meet a future challenge.

- Without rehearsal loss or disaster is even harder to handle. We feel alone and unbalanced.

- Your old concept of yourself and your life has been changed or even shattered.

- This, too, is a story. It's part of the timeless and universal story of death and rebirth.

- In acknowledging your story as a reflection of the myth, you can tap into the power of myth.

- With creative expression and ritual you can be carried by this power to the other side of the myth—renewal. This comes through creation and connection, art and ritual.

Performing your ceremony is step towards re-writing your story. When you decide upon a specific intention, you create a direction for yourself. Involvement with the creative process and undertaking the ceremony moves you toward the future. This passage is a process that will take place over a period of time. The incorporation stage of a rite of passage includes the recognition of a new sense of self and a new status in your society. There is both an internal and an external recognition of your change. This stage, while clearly described, is certainly not defined. If you have the misfortune of becoming a widow or widower, you have the title that describes you as having lost your spouse. People will acknowledge your loss with sympathy and compassion. Initially, the new status is easy to recognize and respond to. But what about six months later? Who are you then and how are you treated? People will wait for your cues to how you would like them to behave and you may not know since you're involved in a process that is changing you.

Incorporating the shifts initiated by your ritual or creative work is somewhat easier. Can you evaluate your inner experience? How would you recognize a difference? What would be a sign? When you designed a ceremony, you first decided upon a specific result you wished to achieve. Did that happen? If not, what do you feel did occur? Sometimes changes are very subtle and occur without any conscious recognition of them. We feel or act differently so naturally that we forget it was not this way before. Imagine a very tall isosceles triangle like the one in the diagram.

Before your passage began you were at the apex of the image, ready to continue straight down the line of life. You experienced a loss and addressed it. The new path, not yet defined, is at first so close to the original that it is difficult to distinguish the difference. Gradually as you continue the journey, the new line separates from the original and becomes clearly distinguishable. This new line is a new story line. It may be a whole new story or a variation on a theme. Only time will tell.

CHAPTER 9

Applications

Withdraw into yourself and look. And if you do not find yourself beautiful yet, act as does the creator of a statue . . . cut away all that is excessive, straighten all that is crooked, bring light to all that is overcast. . . .

—Plotinus

YOU CAN USE your creativity at any time for ceremonies to perform alone. But you can also design and enact ceremonies with a partner, a family, or a group. This chapter has examples from each category that you can adapt for your own use.

INDIVIDUAL RITUALS

Cancer

Bryan, a long distance runner, had been diagnosed with prostate cancer and was undergoing conventional treatment. After years of running he felt very connected to his body; he knew it and himself well. Finding out about the cancer threw him off some and the treatments made him feel very out of touch. *Intention:* Bryan

wanted to reconnect with his body, himself, and his ability to heal. *Planning:* Weakened from the treatments and unable to run he explored more gentle routes to use his body to bring back his over-all health and strength. He decided upon Hatha Yoga. *Preparation:* Bryan bought a book on Hatha Yoga by Yogi Ramacharaka. After reading the book, he laid out a beginning schedule, and cleared a place in his room that would be used only for this purpose. *Manifestation:* Every morning Bryan did his routine. He began with a prayer, then did a series of breathing exercises. These were followed by a period of meditation. After a short break he went through a series of physical exercises and ended it all with a yogi bath. *Incorporation:* The treatments were successful and Bryan was able to begin running again. His new running routine was prefaced by a modified version of the Yoga practice. Bryan found that many of the needs the long running time had served were now being met with Yoga.

Parent with Alzheimer's disease

When Darla found out her father had Alzheimer's she was stunned but relieved. His forgetfulness and confusion had deteriorated to such a degree that the family feared he was going senile. Watching the man who had been so wise and controlled act more like a child had scared her. Where was the strong father she could turn to? *Intention:* Knowing that he would never again be the father she had known, she wanted to accept and love the man he was becoming. *Planning:* Darla went to the library and checked out an armload of books on the disease. She also called his doctor and arranged for a meeting. *Preparation:* After learning as much as possible about the disease and its progression, she culled a number of things she could do with her father at various stages of deterioration. *Manifestation:* Every Saturday Darla went to see her dad just to spend time with him, provide stimulating activities, and try to communicate. She'd enter the house, and later the nursing home saying, "Hi Dad, it's father and daughter day again!" *Incorporation:* These visits proved very rewarding and at the same time, difficult and painful. Darla worked with her therapist to sort out her feelings and find the strength to continue.

Divorce

Mariah had been using ritual to support or celebrate life changes for a number of years. When her marriage dissolved after eight years she knew it would be hard to resolve her feelings and start again even with ritual, but she felt it would be impossible without it. *Intention:* The first step would be acknowledging all the good times the years had given them and saying good-bye to the "we" that shared those experiences. *Planning:* Since she was moving to a new apartment there was a good deal of sorting and separating to do. She found boxes of envelopes filled with photographs that chronicled their married life. Going through the pictures, Mariah decided to make an album as a good-bye to her husband and a letting go for her. *Preparation:* A shopping trip took her to a camera store where she found an oversize album with blank black pages. Next, she went to a stationers for some gold ink pens and glue-on corner tabs. Armed with photographs, supplies, and a pot of tea, she arranged everything on the dining room table and sat down. *Manifestation:* Mariah went through the envelopes looking at the contents and remembering. She culled one or two pictures from each that showed the good times they'd shared with each other, and with friends and family. After gluing these on the pages, she wrote brief memories or comments underneath each picture. On the few blank pages that remained at the end of the album, Mariah wrote a letter to her husband saying good-bye. She found a box in which he'd packed some of his books and placed the finished album on the top, sealing it and leaving it with his things. *Incorporation:* The last year of the marriage had not been good. This project let her find a way to put the past behind her;

she remembered many good times, and acknowledged that it had not all been a mistake.

Car theft

Having your car stolen is a terrifying experience. A car is a big, expensive possession. It's an intimate home away from home that holds many of your personal effects. And a car is expensive to replace. When Don's car was stolen from in front of his house he was frightened and angry. He feared information found in the car would give the thieves even greater access to his personal life and he felt very vulnerable. He also wanted his car back. He paid for it, cared for it, and wanted it. It was obvious that Don had a lot invested in this car, emotionally as well as monetarily. While he couldn't do much to bring back his car, he knew he could and had to do something about how he felt. *Intention:* Don wanted to feel that he and his possessions could be more secure and he wanted to dispel his anger. *Planning:* He decided to personally build a tall redwood fence all around his house. *Preparation:* At the lumber yard, Don found all the materials he'd need along with complete instructions. *Manifestation:* Don did every bit of the labor; all the digging, pouring concrete, sawing, and hammering to make that fence. When it was finished, he had a locksmith install locks on the gates. *Incorporation:* Not only did Don make his house remarkably more secure than it had been before, but he exhausted his anger with the intensive labor.

RITUALS IN RELATIONSHIPS

Infertility

Trevor and Laura had been trying to get pregnant for almost two years when they admitted something might be wrong. Visits to the doctor determined they would not be able to have children.

This was a difficult decree for them. Both had come from large families and having their own offspring was something they had looked forward to. Both felt frustrated and angry at their inability to conceive. They didn't know if they should seek more medical tests and remedies or just give up. *Intention:* They decided it would be best to let go of the desire for biological children and focus on the idea of adoption. *Planning:* Laura felt it was important to spend time with babies to see if they could understand if it was a baby they wanted, or making a baby with their own genetic heritage. They thought the hands-on experience of baby-sitting might provide some insight. *Preparation:* They borrowed a crib from Laura's brother and his wife and set it up in the den. Trevor called his sister who had a three-month-old girl, and Laura called two of her friends who were new mothers. They made the offer of free baby-sitting most evenings and weekends. *Manifestation:* Before long, Laura and Trevor were in the baby-sitting business. Two more babies came from referrals and they had their hands full every weekend. They discovered all babies were lovable and magical beings, no matter who they belonged to. *Incorporation:* While they still felt some grief at not being able to create one of those precious beings, they looked forward to loving an adopted baby one day soon.

Relocation

When Brian got a long-awaited promotion and found the new position would be in another state, Gary knew he'd have to leave his less meaningful job to follow a more meaningful relationship. Over the years they had developed many strong friendships and felt the most difficult aspect of the move would be leaving their family-like community. *Intention:* Gary and Brian wanted to say good-bye to their friends in a really special way. *Planning:* They chose to have a big party at which they would present a meaningful gift to each guest. Gary was an artist and wanted to make personalized collages for everyone. Brian had the idea of having a dinner where everyone ate from the same bowl to symbolize the support they felt from their friends. Everything had to be video-taped. *Preparation:* While Gary cut out hundreds of pictures from magazines and arranged them, along with drawings and comments on constructed cards to characterize each person, Brian called an Ethiopian restaurant for instructions and catering. *Manifestation:* Everyone gathered in the living room which was glowing with countless candles. A loud gong quieted the crowd and Bryan directed the guests to sit in a circle around a huge tablecloth. In the center of the cloth was a giant tray with meats and vegetables soaking into a pancake-like bread called injera. There were also plates of injera set around the platter. Eating entailed taking a piece of the bread and reaching into the center to scoop up some fillings. The meal turned out to be delicious, messy, and hilarious. When everyone was sated and cleaned up, the gifts were presented. This, too, was rather uproarious and at the same time quite poignant. *Incorporation:* There were many fond memories of that party. The tape helped "bring them back home" until a new home was established.

Loss of pet

Bonnie and Ernie never had any children, but they had lots of cats over the years. In addition to at least three cats of their own they always fed the neighborhood strays. When their cat, Sweetie, had to be put to sleep they were very upset. *Intention:* They wanted to hold a funeral for Sweetie and give her an honorable burial. *Planning:* Because they lived in an apartment they asked their niece Rochelle who had been their long time cat-sitter if the event could take place in her back yard. *Preparation:* Bonnie and Ernie put Sweetie's favorite toys into the box with her body which they'd brought back from the animal hospital. They wrapped the box in a pillowcase and brought it to Rochelle's. Sweetie's vet had sent a really beautiful sympathy card that had the perfect poem for the eulogy. *Manifestation:* Rochelle and her boyfriend had prepared a place in the corner of the flower bed. Ernie set Sweetie's box into the earth and Bonnie read the piece from the card. Each put a shovel full of earth into the hole and Ernie completed the burial. Rochelle had been saving some pretty rocks she'd found on a vacation. They made a circle around the grave with the rocks. When the burial was finished they all went inside for tea and cat stories. *Incorporation:* Bonnie and Ernie still missed their cat, but they felt much better knowing she was safely interred in a spot they could visit.

Retirement

Marta was a dedicated teacher who worked with second graders for the past twenty-five years. Now, nearing fifty-five, she was ready to leave teaching and join her husband who retired from his job a year earlier. Maceo found out retirement was not the same as a vacation. It required adjusting to a whole new lifestyle. He wanted to use what he had learned to make it easier for Marta. After thirty years of marriage, Maceo sensed the most difficult step for Marta would be leaving the children. He had heard there would be a party for her and called around to see if he could facilitate the event. *Intention:* Maceo wanted to find ways for Marta's colleagues and students to acknowledge her value as a caring, creative teacher and help her say good-bye to a rewarding career. *Planning:* Working together with Marta's teaching assistant, Liz, Maceo came up with a plan. Liz had large cardboard cut-outs of the letters of the alphabet. Maceo would send three letters to each teacher asking them to come up with qualities describing Marta that begin with each of the letters. They could write or draw on the cardboard, or otherwise decorate it. Liz would contact the parents of the children in Marta's class and ask them to have their sons and daughters draw a good-bye picture for her. *Preparation:* Liz made a book from all the children's letters and wrote her own letter which she glued to the cover. Maceo collected the cardboard cut-outs and strung them together. *Manifestation:* Teachers, students, parents, and the principal came to the party to present Marta with the gifts and express both their appreciation and their sadness. Maceo had his own gift for Marta, tickets for a long-awaited trip to Europe. *Incorporation:* Marta and Maceo spent weeks traveling together, rediscovering life and each other.

FAMILY RITUALS

Addiction

Richard was an alcoholic. His parents had been alcoholics and his father had died of alcohol-related problems. But if you called Richard an alcoholic, he'd deny it. He only drank beer. The problem was, Richard drank beer almost all day long. He would have a couple of beers at lunch, a beer or two before dinner, one with dinner, and then maybe he'd go out for drinks. Over time he developed a tolerance so it wasn't obvious he was high until late in the evening. What his friends, family, and co-workers could tell, was that Richard was not the man they once knew. Saturday through Monday he'd wake up sick and hung over. He was short-tempered and unreliable. His children were afraid to make any noise and his wife was worried. She'd tried talking with him many times but met with a wall of denial. It was obvious something had to be done to prevent the progression of his alcoholism before it destroyed him and everyone around him.

Intention: Richard's wife Lola, talked with close friends and family members and they decided to do a positive intervention with the aid of an addictions counselor. *Planning:* Lola and the people she'd spoken with, along with a few of Richard's buddies from work, set up a meeting with a counselor from a local center.

Preparation: Together with the counselor they structured an intervention that would include loving confrontation, a complete plan for treatment, and answers to any and all objections. After two meetings they were ready to talk to Richard. *Manifestation:* Everyone met in a neutral space and Richard was brought in by a friend. They all sat down and guided by the counselor, took turns telling Richard how he'd been acting, how his behavior had made them feel, and that they cared about him and wanted him to get better. This was a very difficult process for everyone involved, but by the end Richard agreed to go into treatment. *Incorporation:* During Richard's treatment program and for a very long time after, everyone made sure to be as supportive as possible. They learned about the disease from the counselor. Some of his friends and family joined him at his meetings and became aware of how their actions could be harmful or helpful in aiding Richard maintain sobriety.

Death of a grandparent

Seven-year-old Jake and his five-year-old sister Beth had been very close to their grandfather. They were Hy's only grandchildren and they spent lots of time together. When he was diagnosed with a terminal illness, his family was more solicitous then ever. Hy enjoyed his grandchildren and always was cheered when they were present. His death, although expected, was still a shock. He'd been sick for so long, it seemed that was just the way it was. Everyone missed him dearly, but the children awaited his return. It's difficult for young children to comprehend death. They'd ask their mother, Linda, when Grandpa would be back. This made it even harder for her to deal with the loss. *Intention:* Linda and her husband, Scott, felt it was important to do something for the children and for themselves to say good-bye to Grandpa without completely losing him. *Planning:* They decided it was best to say Grandpa would not really ever come back, and at the same time show how Grandpa's love, thoughts, and feelings remained. *Preparation:*

They found pictures of the family that had been taken with Hy when he had been up and about, and put them into heart-shaped frames. *Manifestation:* Sunday morning they called everyone into the kitchen for breakfast. Linda had made pancakes, Hy's favorite breakfast. "Who's favorite breakfast is this?" "Grandpa's," they both answered. "And what does Grandpa like on his pancakes?" Linda continued. "Honey," answered Jake, "and that's what I want." "Me, too!" chimed in Beth. During the meal Linda and Scott talked about Grandpa. They said he would always be in their hearts and they could remember him and talk about him any time. Scott brought out the pictures and asked the children to find good places for each one. *Incorporation:* Linda and Scott made it a point to talk about Grandpa frequently, especially if they were doing something the children had done with him or associated with him. Jake invited Grandma to join in their rememberings as well.

Job loss

Marcus was thrilled when he got promoted to manager of a health club. He'd been at the new location from the beginning and with the organization for over two years. This meant changes for his family, too. His wife, Terry could cut back her hours at the youth center and put more energy into her painting. Everything was better than they'd hoped; then the rumors started. The company was selling the club at that location to another organization. Yesterday's rumors became tomorrow's reality. Marcus lost his job.

It was easy for Terry to cut her hours but going back to full-time would be difficult, and they'd have to put their daughter Ariel back in an after school program. The worst part was finding a new job before the money ran out. As skilled as Marcus was, jobs were hard to come by. He knew he could earn some money as a personal trainer but that would be an interim means. *Intention:* They knew they'd have to budget and wanted to find a creative way to cut back that would keep them from feeling deprived. *Planning:*

The family looked at all the things they spent money on for entertainment or frivolously. Terry and Marcus also looked at money paid to other people to do what they could do themselves. They decided to do as many of these things as possible as a family. ***Preparation:*** Terry painted weekly calendars on large pieces of newsprint. Everyone filled in the days with plans and responsibilities. Then, they made daily and weekly lists for all the little details. ***Manifestation:*** Friday night began the week for them. That was when they decided what the meals would be, who would cook, and who would pack lunches. When this was finished they'd watch a video together. On Saturday morning they'd take care of the yard, wash the cars, or do the laundry (things they had previously paid others to do.) ***Incorporation:*** Marcus was a good trainer and a good manager. The positive support from his family and the results he helped his clients achieve kept him hopeful and confident. His networking was successful and Marcus was able to make it until another job came through.

Adolescence

Leon was changing so much he barely recognized himself. He'd grown three inches in the last year, his voice was changing, and there was hair growing in new places on his body. He had been preparing for his Bar Mitzvah for the past two months, but he did not feel his studying was helping him become a man. In fact, his Jewish identity seemed really separate from his life outside of his home. Leon's friend Noah had a really cool ceremony that his father made up with his men's drumming group. ***Intention:*** Leon wanted a ceremony that he made up himself that would give his family a chance to see and help with his changes. ***Planning:*** He talked with his dad, Ben, about being a man. Ben offered to take Leon on a two-week camping trip to Black Rock Desert in northwest Nevada. They would take the four-wheel drive and go to a desolate area where it would be just the two of them. Leon thought it would be great to backpack and camp, and maybe even learn to drive. *Preparation:* The "guys" went together to the camping store and bought all kinds of equipment and supplies. Ben was a seasoned camper and already had a tent and most of the other necessary gear. Leon made it clear that his mother and sister were not supposed to help them get ready, nor were they to ask a bunch of questions when he and his dad returned. They would tell them what they felt like telling, when they felt like talking about it. *Manifestation:* Ben and Leon spent a glorious two weeks in nature, learning about the land, fishing, soaking in hot springs, with no rules or schedule. Leon was an equal partner on the trip. *Incorporation:* After the trip and the Bar Mitzvah, Leon realized he had changed in more ways than he'd suspected. It was obvious to everyone that he was more confident.

GROUP OR COMMUNITY RITUALS

Natural disaster

After the devastating fire of October 20, 1991 that consumed much of the Oakland and Berkeley hills, killing twenty-five people and destroying over 3,000 homes, many in the community were moved to act. Ruth Block, a local artist, knew she had to get involved. *Intention:* With her energy driving the project, an organization was born to coordinate all the community and individual responses to the fire and aftermath into a comprehensive exhibition and series of events to be held simultaneously at different locations throughout Berkeley and Oakland. This would take place over approximately one month surrounding the one year anniversary of the disaster. The exhibition and events would commemorate, document, and provide a vehicle for the community to heal from, overcome, and transcend disaster. *Planning:* A series of meetings were held to discuss details and form committees. *Preparation:* Artists' information and applications for submission sheets were drawn up and distributed. Donations were solicited. Venues were secured. Volunteers encouraged even more volunteers to help with printed materials, advertising, and mailings. A considerable amount of art from hundred of contributors was collected, reviewed, and placed. Schedules were drawn up. Press releases went out. A rehearsal for the main event was held and finally, all was in place on schedule. *Manifestation:* Forty different locations exhibited original paintings, graphics, photo collages, poetry, and dramatic writings that were done by children and adults from all over the Bay area. Both amateurs and professionals contributed. The main event held in an auditorium on the edge of Oakland's Lake Merritt, featured a performance by a group of women on stilts who enacted the firestorm through dance. There were several powerful videos shown, and a number of readings, some heartbreaking, some simply touching. Music, a ritual, poster and book signings and sales, and food and drink rounded things out. *Incorporation:* The community cooperation and spirit fostered by this event was very strong. All the work, especially the events and exhibitions, helped honor and acknowledge people's feelings through public display and acceptance.

Crime

After the shooting on Jefferson street everyone was talking to each other for a change. Neighbors who in the past hadn't even nodded were now having conversations. A group of neighbors informally gathered in one of the parking areas and someone suggested a Home Alert meeting. *Intention:* The idea seemed worth pursuing. Someone volunteered to contact the police department for more information, and someone else promised to call on the nearby church to see if they could hold a meeting there. Everyone promised to get back together at the same time in three days. *Planning:* There were seven people at the next get-together and work for all of them. A police officer would come on the fourteenth of the month. *Preparation:* The church would have to be notified of the date. One woman offered to make up fliers at work, and the others agreed to distribute them to all the apartments on the block. *Manifestation:* Over half the tenants on the block showed up for the meeting. They learned how to make their neighborhood safer by following a number of easy steps. One person volunteered to chair a monthly meeting where people could check in, meet each other, share new information, and begin to form a tighter community. Someone suggested including some of the surrounding blocks. Another person volunteered to have a "hotline." Those who felt comfortable exchanged phone numbers. *Incorporation:* Although these people lived in a rather transient neighborhood, they were able to establish a kind of core group that met each month. New people or old members would show up from time to time and get updated on what was going on. People took much more responsibility for the neighborhood and were more friendly and cooperative than before.

Death of a public figure

In late November of 1978, former San Francisco Supervisor Dan White shot and killed two political figures in City Hall offices. One was Mayor George Moscone, the other, Supervisor Harvey Milk, was a leader of the city's gay population. On the evening of the assassination close to thirty thousand people walked from down Market Street in San Francisco to City Hall in a candlelight procession.

Candlelight vigils or processions are used to mark the passing of someone that holds importance to a community or to show support for a specific issue. *Intention:* Generally a group exists that is aligned with the person or issue, or one is immediately formed in response to need. *Planning:* Members of the group choose a leader, select a time and date for the event, determine the meeting spot and necessary logistics, and pick a potential speaker or speakers. *Preparation:* The group then prints and tacks up hundreds of posters announcing the event, distributes thousands of fliers on the streets, and sends out as many press releases and public service announcements as possible. They may also contact performers who are well-known as an added draw. Candles and holders must be bought and disposition planned. *Manifestation:* As people arrived they are greeted and offered long candles that may be poked through Styrofoam cups or paper drip catchers. Later donations will be requested. When a good number of people have gathered, speeches are given, songs are sung, and when the energy is high the procession begins. Silently or accompanied by chants or song, the group solemnly walks to their destination. There, more speeches and other activities occur, until the energy winds down and is capped with a closing speech. *Incorporation:* Sometimes the intention of this kind of ceremony involves getting attention for an ideology or cause. Notice by the media and follow-up outreach work would be indicated as part of the incorporation process. In other instances the intention is to build a community where people can share their feelings and find support. Incorporation would then be done both on a personal level by each participant, and by the organizing group to evaluate their success.

Closing of a company

The Mosley Company, established on the East Coast in the early 1900s, had a family feeling to it, even with four hundred employees. Once a solid contender in the manufacture of baby carriages, competition with foreign manufacturing prices, rising liability rates, and increased shipping costs were eating at the foundation of the business. Finally, the owners were forced to sell the business to a huge corporation. *Intention:* Although there was really no way to make this an easy transition, the owners wanted to offer their employees as much support and assistance as possible by hearing their needs and ideas and providing whatever they could to help. *Planning:* The owners passed out questionnaires to the employees asking for suggestions about how to ease the transition. These were discussed at a company-wide meeting and the ideas that were feasible in terms of resources, time, and energy were separated out for implementation. *Preparation:* The best idea was to hire a transition management team. They decided that this should be done immediately. *Manifestation:* The team worked with the company for a month, providing psychological and career counseling, occupational therapy, and other specifics that were needed. In addition a final potluck was scheduled for the week before the actual plant closing. Employees and their families all gathered to say good-bye, and receive letters of acknowledgment and recommendation. *Incorporation:* Many of the ideas set in motion by the transition team were developed and carried out over the subsequent weeks and months. Many of the employees continued to meet for career counseling sessions and emotional support.

CHAPTER 10

Anniversaries

Ah, love, let us be true to one another....
... the world which seems
To lie before us like a land of dreams
So various, so beautiful, so new,
Hath really neither joy, nor love, nor light,
Nor certitude, nor peace, nor help from pain;
And we are here as on a darkling plain
Swept with confused alarms of struggle and flight,
Where ignorant armies clash by night.

—Matthew Arnold, "Dover Beach"

All passages occur over time. The overwhelming feelings of grief that predominated after the death of my father eventually receded as other experiences that composed my life demanded my attention. After the first three months passed I knew I would eventually be okay. Then I was unexpectedly thrown back into despair when the anniversary of his birth came around. I would not have flown back to Chicago to spend the day with him had he still been alive, yet I felt an extraordinary sadness at the realization that

I would no longer have the option to celebrate his birthday with him ever again. Each time an important day approached, birthdays of my sisters, my mother, or my own, my parent's wedding anniversary, and certain holidays, I was reminded again that the last celebration had been the last.

It's important to do something symbolic around birthdays, anniversaries, and holidays. I spent an afternoon at Vesper Hospice in San Leandro learning how they addressed this dilemma. "Hospice is a comprehensive program of care for people in the final stages of a life-threatening illness. It allows patients to remain as comfortable and active as possible in their homes, surrounded and cared for by family and friends. The Hospice team visits the patient and family, anywhere from once a month to several times a week, depending on patient and family needs."[1] In addition to emotional support and counseling they offer bereavement counseling and support groups. Nancy Sobanya, bereavement counselor, and Cheryl Richards, coordinator of the Kids, Teens, and Loss program, shared how they honor the deceased and the survivors at these difficult times.

Twice a year their agency holds an Evening of Remembrance. This ecumenical memorial service is attended by family members who have participated in the program in the past year. The memorial begins with the chaplain doing a reading as an invocation. Then she relates a story of her own loss and invites people to stand and share their losses. The officiant then reads the names of the people who have died and with each name the family members go to the altar to light candles in memory. Each person is given a flower after lighting a candle. All the families are asked to bring photographs or mementos of their loved one to place on the richly decorated altar. Everyone joins in singing a series of songs: "The Rose," "Amazing Grace," "You'll Never Walk Alone," "Morning Has Broken," and "Wind Beneath the Wings." Poems are read, too. One in particular, "We Remember Them," has places for response. This ceremony provides family members with a personal and public acknowledgment of their grief, and of the life and death of their loved one.

Nancy and Cheryl also recommend writing a letter or sending a card to a deceased friend or family member, visiting the grave, going to dinner in their honor, or finding some way to celebrate the person's life. These acts are positive ways to express the feelings that arise, and are opportunities to handle unfinished business.

It's never too late to say good-bye. Whether you have lost someone you care about to death, divorce, a move, a fight, or the ability to be fully conscious, you can still communicate with them in some fashion. Your loss may require completion with someone who has harmed you in some way. It could even be a part of your own body, your youth, or a memory. Whatever you have lost, a person, place, object, idea, or principle, it may not be over for you. Even if you thought the severance itself or the initial grieving was the end, you may have more words and more feelings about your loss. The anniversary of the event can summon these feelings. Other anniversaries associated with the experience or the aftermath can also be evocative.

Sometimes it takes a long time to gain strength to face a loss. Whenever feelings come up, it's good to have resources to deal with them. Creative expression and ritual, family and community support, and a connection with Spirit can be there for you. If you initially experienced your loss as a source of confusion or pain, perhaps this was all you could manage at the time. An anniversary often serves to reawaken the loss. Many people respond by turning to spiritual practices and deepening their sense of connection on all levels.

A very old symbolic system further depicts this. The Tarot is a deck of seventy-eight cards, twenty-two of them are known as major arcana. These correspond to fundamental expressions of energy common to all, as well as basic challenges that must be met for growth. The twelfth card, the hanged man, represents surrender. One guidebook uses a discussion by Carl Jung to describe this condition. as "... a boundless expanse full of unprecedented uncertainty, with apparently no inside and no outside, no above and no below, no here and no there, no mine and no thine, no good and no bad. It is the world of water where all life floats in suspension."[2] Once you meet the challenge of this card and let go, you move to the next step along the path which is represented by the death card. This card is one of the three paths that lead from ego awareness to awareness of higher self. Its meaning is a fear of annihilation and resistance to giving up. But once surrender of your old way of being has been accepted, you pass through a gateway and are reborn to a higher level.

No one wants to remain bewildered, angry, helpless, or in pain. There is a saying that goes, "When the student is ready the teacher will come." Many people have reported coincidental or synchronistic events occurring that helped them just when they needed it. The following stories are just a few examples that show how this can happen.

Renee's mother had painfully succumbed to cancer the year before, and Renee had planned to plant a permanent memorial in her garden for the first anniversary of the death. She chose baby's tears and mother ferns, plants that had been important to her mother. As the day of the anniversary came closer Renee began having vivid memories of the days preceding her mother's death. By the eve of the anniversary, Renee's emotional state was nearly out of control. She began to pray desperately for help. The next morning as she stood on the deck in her yard, she heard a loud flapping sound. A big white blob flew past and landed somewhere down the hill. Renee ran down the path in search of the object. There was nothing to be found in the lower garden. "Oh well," she thought, "since I'm out here I might as well look for a spot for the plants." The search was appearing to be unproductive when, again, she heard the sound of flapping in a tree above her. It was a huge white duck, and it was flying up to her yard. As she climbed back up to find the duck she passed "the spot." After digging some holes for the plants, Renee went back toward the house. The beautiful wild duck was just sitting there, waiting for her and quacking. It stayed all day, then flew off as mysteriously as it had arrived.

Another story involves Buck, a man who was the youngest of eight children. He left his family after high school, never having felt a part of the family. He changed his name and moved across the country. Years passed and he had very little contact with his siblings or his parents who were by now getting on in years. In a rare phone call home, he learned his father was not well. Twenty years had passed. Buck was nearing forty and re-evaluating his life. He decided to quit his dead-end job. Filled with dreams of a better future he looked for a career, and then just a job, with no success. As a last resort he called his parents hoping they'd make him a temporary loan. Instead, they invited him back to live and offered him an apartment, work, and opportunity. He flew back to make arrangements and discovered a large warm, welcoming family, all sincerely wanting him home.

If you break open
The cherry tree
Where are the
flowers?
But in the springtime,
See how they bloom!
— Ikkyu, 15th Century Japanese poet

Anniversaries can be opportunities in disguise. They provide measures by which you can evaluate the process of your transition. As an anniversary approaches you may find yourself feeling out of sorts. Some people get depressed or irritable and don't know where the feelings are coming from. Use creative expression at these times to make an assessment of your emotional state and to move forward.

A Bay area resident I'll call Zora depicts one type of response. In early October of 1992 Zora began having nightmares. She would awaken suddenly, bathed in sweat, heart pounding, feeling like she was trying to escape from some horribly threatening force. The year before Zora had escaped a disaster. Her home was one of several that remained standing in an area where most properties were burned to the ground. Although she remained in the neighborhood and watched the new buildings going up and the land turning green something in her did not feel the threat was over. Maybe the same fire wouldn't return, but another fire could surely be in wait, ready to turn into a massive conflagration.

Fortunately many groups were available to help the victims of that fire, and Zora joined with others of the neighborhood and community who felt the need to give and receive support.

Frank, a stroke victim, had a different type of anniversary experience. Frank found it very difficult to adjust emotionally as well as physically to his paralysis. His physical therapist tried the traditional forms of rehabilitation with little success. He was just too depressed. One day Frank entered the therapy room just as she was finishing up with a child. "Why not use the same materials with Frank?" she thought. His introduction to this new procedure began with modeling clay. At first he just squeezed it listlessly. Soon he realized he enjoyed the feel of the warm, pliable clay and begin to shape it. Gradually he regained motor control in his damaged hand and arm. Each finished piece was whisked away by the therapist and stored in a safe place. When three months had passed, the therapist brought all of Frank's pieces out and displayed them. The progress was quite obvious and he felt heartened for the first time. He allowed her to draw up a timetable to check his development in monthly increments and agreed to work on other parts of his body as well.

There is no way to predict how an impending anniversary will affect you. Knowing that you may experience uncomfortable feelings can be helpful. In another area of my work I have helped people with smoking cessation. I warn them that after they quit smoking they may experience cravings for cigarettes one month, three, six, or twelve months later. When people quit drugs or alcohol they may have sudden cravings years later. Sometimes there are triggers that precipitate the cravings. When you are aware that certain feelings and behaviors are possible you can prepare or intervene in appropriate ways.

Preparation includes having an available support system that you know you can call on, or a practice you can return to. Interventions like the ideas presented in chapter seven can be effective when you have a sense of what you're dealing with. It's important to hold on to your own truth about your feelings. You may have the experience of being invalidated if you share what's going on with you. Even well meaning friends can say you don't know what you're feeling, or there's no reason to feel that way. *Don't listen to them.* While you may have little desire to hold on to a depression, denying or ignoring your feelings will not work. Acknowledge what you feel even if it makes no sense, is not pleasant, or not timely.

Use the same means of dealing with your feelings as you did before. If something worked before, try it again. If that intervention isn't effective, try another approach. Your loss has created a change in you. Perhaps something that you couldn't do before is right for you now.

There's also the chance that you've changed a great deal. You may have the good fortune to discover that as an anniversary approaches, there is no longer any energy in it for you. While memory of the experience is intact, there is no emotional charge. May it be so.

CHAPTER II

Death

The Ancient sages saw the Universe as an eternal ritual of sacrifice. It is the self-sacrifice of the Absolute which gives birth to the relative and the very nature of life is one of transformation of energies. Every aspect of creation, divine or human, reflects this transformation.

We cannot live without taking part in this ritual, both as instrument and as victims, and it is through his conscious participation in the sacrificial ritual that cosmic order is maintained.

—Brihad Aranyaka Upanishad

SOCIETIES AROUND THE world and throughout history have developed belief systems to understand and deal with death. These include practices of caring for and disposing of the deceased, and rituals that give social support for grief and mourning. "Traces of pollen discovered in burial caves in northern Iraq indicate that Neanderthal communities put flowers on the graves of their dead. So with bouquets of flowers or gravestones of marble, humankind

has probably been marking the final resting places of loved ones for at least 30,000 years."[1] The United States is a country filled with people of many different cultures. Even those of us who have been here for generations may still be influenced by the traditions and beliefs of our ancestors. At the same time we are fortunate to have many other traditions to draw from and incorporate into our own belief systems.

Each year, San Francisco's Mission District celebrates a Mexican tradition known as Days of the Dead. October 31 through November 2 are the days when the souls of the dead are believed to return to Earth. Family members assemble elaborate household altars called *ofrendas* and prepare special foods in honor of the visits. At sundown on November 1, the families go to the cemeteries for an all-night watch and communion with the dead. Candles are lit on the gravestones to commemorate each soul, and the hundreds of lights illuminate the scene throughout the night.

At the Galeria de la Raza, what began as a small gathering has grown to enormous proportions over the years. People of many cultures gather to participate in the candlelight procession of *Dia de los Muertos*. Churches, stores, schools, and private homes have shrines displaying photographs of the deceased, flowers, food, personal items, and candles that they've set up in the windows along the route. The walk ends in front of a large mural painted on an outside wall of the Galeria, where participants stand and talk with each other about death and life.

Death is no stranger in San Francisco where the AIDS epidemic has taken many young lives. Perhaps this contributes to so many creative responses being born to help with the processes of dying and bereavement. The Ghia Art Gallery "began as a retail casket and urn outlet and educational resource ... with a goal to shift public attitudes on death away from the morbid, impersonal and expensive prevailing practices, to something more creative, life affirming and low cost. ..."[2] They offer many traditional and nontraditional options for burial planning that give people more opportunities to express their personal feelings. Ghia representative, Maria told me this somewhat unorthodox story: "One family came here and painted the cardboard box used to hold the body as it goes into the retort for cremation. They all brought paints and decorated the whole box."

Acting alone and acting with others are vital means of coping with grief. In San Francisco's Golden Gate Park, another opportunity for people to express and transform their feelings was initiated by four survivors of AIDS victims. The AIDS Memorial Grove is "an ongoing project to create a living memorial in memory of people lost to AIDS. . . . One Saturday each month, volunteers are invited to help with the work of creating the Grove. . . . Workdays not only provide the means of renovating . . . the site, . . . they have become a special time of hope and renewal, allowing a positive focus for concern and grief."[3]

The Bay Area is not the only location where people have found creative ways to mobilize their grief. "The Vietnam War Memorial in Washington, D.C., provides an ongoing healing ritual as family members and friends who lost men and women in the war come, find their person's name on the wall, and make rubbings to carry back home, thus affirming their own personal loss while connecting with a larger community. Such trips to the wall are often referred to as 'pilgrimages.'"[4]

Groups and communities pool resources, strengths, and energy to bring more than could be expected to the healing process. Young people at the Creative Learning Center in Austin, Texas write letters to deceased friends and relatives to complete unfinished business and cope with their loss. Some of them have taken this a step further through a group they call The Cultural Warriors. By turning the letters into skits, they commemorate the dead and develop skills to manage issues facing the living.

Death is the key to the door of life.
—Elizabeth Kübler-Ross, *Death, The Final Stage of Growth*

Dealing with unfinished business or an unresolved conflict is the first issue that must be confronted after a death. When a good friend back in Chicago died of a heart attack just three weeks after his forty-fifth birthday, the pain of loss that I experienced was exacerbated by an overwhelming sense of guilt. "I could have told him I loved him, if only I had made that birthday call," I lamented repeatedly. My sisters who promised to be my emissaries at the funeral assured me I was mistaken. He had mentioned recently speaking to me. Somehow, as much as I longed to release my guilt, I never fully believed them. I knew it was my responsibility to say good-bye and did so in a structured meditation. After making a conscious effort to communicate with my friend's spirit and share all my feelings, I felt greatly relieved.

Honoring the deceased, appeasing or binding them, or finding symbolic ways to realize unfulfilled wishes of theirs is important to many. These needs can be satisfied by burying or burning certain items along with the body. One woman who was pregnant with her first child lost her mother just months before the baby's birth. She obtained a hollow boulder with a memorial plate for her mother's ashes, along with permission to leave the remains in a nearby state park. After the birth, she buried the placenta under the boulder. One month later the family held a naming ceremony in the park: here the baby was given her grandmother's name.

In your body ... are the two cosmic forces: that which destroys, and that which creates. ... Yes, in your body are all things that exist in the three worlds (of earth, sky and heaven), all performing their prescribed functions. ... He alone who knows this is held to be a true yogi.
—Jean Varene, *Yoga and the Hindu Tradition*

"Death ends a life but it does not end a relationship, which struggles on in the survivor's mind toward some resolution which it may never find." So begins the movie, *I Never Sang For My Father.* Perhaps adaptation is a more feasible goal than resolution. Once the burial or cremation has taken place and your loved one is physically gone, you are left with an enormous task. Your feelings, while in many ways universal, will be experienced uniquely. There will be times when you will not understand what you are feeling or doing. Take time to discover exactly what you need. I worked with two women who had recently lost their fathers. Both were metamorphosing into the roles of independent women from the previous roles of fathers' daughters. Yet each had a different need with respect to her loss. For Karen, it was unfinished business. She needed to release unexpressed anger felt toward her father. For Gayla, her father's death meant the loss of an important relationship that would never be there again. The ritual we designed for Karen was more of a healing ceremony. Karen was very articulate and expressed herself easily on paper. She decided to write her father a long letter, verbalizing her feelings. Using red watercolor paint and watercolor paper, she spent several days filling many sheets of paper with her sad angry words. When she was finished we brought the papers and a large wash bowl filled with water outside. There Karen invoked the spirit of her father and tearfully read the letter. Afterwards she soaked the pages in the water, letting the pages wash clean while the water turned blood red. This symbolized release and finality. She then took the water to pour over a new tree she had planted—a symbol for possibility and new growth now available.

Gayla's ritual had a completely different tone. I had her bring in a box of photographs of her father and the two of them together, as well as any cards she could find that they had sent to each other. She was also to write up any special memories she had of him. Gayla constructed a memento box that was very much like a treasure chest. She glued photographs to index cards and wrote something special about each picture. Each card was put into categories according to the occasion or the kind of feeling that accompanied the memory. After working on this project for a number of weeks, Gayla came to realize she need never lose the special things she had shared with her father.

You and I are a mountain of grief....
You and I will never meet.
Only try at midnight to send me
A greeting through the stars.
    —Anna Akhmatova, "In a Dream"

If you have recently lost someone you care about to death, any kind of death, focus on your relationship with them and work on release or closure of some sort. You may be in so much pain that you feel like giving up. On a deeper level, what you really want is for everything to be right again, to be whole. That is your intention, to find wholeness. You are not yourself, and so you have the opportunity to remake yourself. Maybe you can begin now. Imagine the sun the way it would look in a drawing. Now see it as if it were three dimensional, a huge glowing orb with warm, golden rays streaming in every direction, rays that extend forever.

Imagine that this sun is Spirit or God, and the rays are our individual spirits. This means that you are a ray of the Great Spirit. We are all rays of the Great Spirit. You will begin to feel that light around you and within you. That warm, golden, healing light can be there more and more as you do this meditation. Sit in the sunlight when you do it. Do it every day. Imagine that you can discern the glow of the sun in others, too. The light is everywhere. When the sun rises each morning, it comes out of the darkness. You can too.

What we call the beginning is often the end
And to make an end is to make a beginning.
The end is where we start from.
                    —T. S. Eliot, *Four Quartets*

ITHAKA
by C. P. Cavafy

As you set out for Ithaka
hope your road is a long one,
full of adventure, full of discovery.
Laistrygonians, Cyclops,
angry Poseidon—don't be afraid of them:
you'll never find things like that on your way
as long as you keep your thoughts raised high,
as long as a rare excitement
stirs your spirit and your body.
Laistrygonians, Cyclops,
wild Poseidon—you won't encounter them
unless you bring them along inside your soul,
unless your soul sets them up in front of you.

Hope your road is a long one.
May there be many summer mornings when,
with what pleasure, what joy,
you enter harbors you're seeing for the first time;
may you stop at Phoenician trading stations,
to buy fine things,
mother of pearl and coral, amber and ebony,
sensual perfumes of every kind—
as many sensual perfumes as you can;
and may you visit many Egyptian cities
to learn and go on learning from their scholars.

Keep Ithaka always in your mind.
Arriving there is what you're destined for.
But don't hurry the journey at all.

Better if it last for years,
so you're old by the time you reach the island,
wealthy with all you've gained on the way,
not expecting Ithaka to make you rich.

Ithaka gave you the marvelous journey.
Without her you wouldn't have set out.
She has nothing else left to give you now.

And if you find her poor, Ithaka won't have fooled you.
Wise as you will have become, so full of experience,
you'll have understood by then what these Ithakas mean.

Support groups and self-help groups are available to help you for just about every imaginable situation. When you approach a local or national group that specializes in helping people with specific needs, be confident that you can benefit from the relationship. Occasionally a group may have a different philosophical orientation than you are comfortable with, or the people in your local chapter may for some reason not be the best match for you. If this should happen you can still draw from their experience as is appropriate and use it elsewhere.

You can find many resources through *The Encyclopedia of Associations,* edited by Peggy Kneffel Daniels and Carol A. Schwartz (Detroit, MI: Gale Research, 1993). These will be in your public library, where you can also discover many other helpful materials.

Following is a short list of resources.

Abuse
Parents Anonymous
520 S. Lafayette Park Place, Suite 316
Los Angeles, CA 90057

Aging
American Senior Citizens Association
P.O. Box 41
Fayetteville, NC 28302

Children of Aging Parents
Woodburne Office Campus,
Suite 302A
1609 Woodburne Road
Levittown, PA 19057

Gray Panthers
1424 16th St. N.W., Suite 602
Washington, D.C. 20036

AIDS

AIDS Project Los Angeles
3670 Wilshire Blvd., Suite 300
Los Angeles, CA 90010

Mothers of AIDS Patients
(M.A.P.)
P.O. Box 1763
Lomita, CA 90717

National Association of People
With AIDS
1012 14th St. NW, Suite 601
Washington, DC

Alcoholism

Alcoholics Anonymous
local chapters are everywhere

Arthritis

Arthritis Foundation
1314 Spring St. NW
Atlanta, GA 30309

Alzheimer's

Alzheimer's Disease
International
919 N. Michigan Ave., #1000
Chicago, IL 60611

Blindness

National Federation of the
Blind
1800 Johnson St.
Baltimore, MD 21230

Cancer

Candlelighters
123 C St. S.E.
Washington, DC 20003

Share and Care
Cancer Education Coordinator
North Memorial Medical
Center
3220 Lowry Ave. N.
Minneapolis, MN 55422

American Cancer Society
1599 Clifton Rd. NE
Atlanta, CA 30329

Missing children

Find the Children
11811 W. Olympic Blvd.
Los Angeles, CA 90064

Crime victims

National Organization for
Victim Assistance (NOVA)
717 D St. N.W.
Washington, DC 20004

National Victim Center
307 W. 7th St., Suite 1001
Fort Worth, TX 76102

Guardian Angels
982 E. 89th St.
Brooklyn, NY 11236

Deafness
Hear Center
301 E. Del Mar Blvd.
Pasadena, CA 91101

Depression
Depressives Anonymous
329 E. 62nd St.
New York, NY 10021

Disfigurement
National Association for the
Craniofacially Handicapped
P.O. Box 11082
Chattanooga, TN 37461

Down's syndrome
National Association for Down's
Syndrome
P.O. Box 4542
Oak Brook, IL 60522

Disability
Amputees in Motion
P.O. Box 2703
Escondido, CA 92033

Goodwill Industries of America
9200 Wisconsin Ave.
Bethesda, MD 20814

Euthanasia
Hemlock Society
P.O. Box 11830
Eugene, OR 94744

Grief
Grief Education
2422 S. Downing St.
Denver, CO 80210

Parents Without Partners
7910 Woodmont Ave.
Washington, DC 20014

Heart attack
Mended Hearts
721 Huntington Ave.
Boston, MA 02115

Hospice
National Hospice Organization
1901 N. Fort Mayer Dr., Suite
402
Arlington, VA 22209

Incest
Survivors of Incest Anonymous
P. O. Box 21817
Baltimore, MD 21222

Infertility
National Infertility Network
Exchange
c/o Ilene Stargot
P. O. Box 204
East Meadow, NY 11554

Mastectomy
Reach to Recovery
c/o American Cancer Society
1599 Clifton Rd. NE
Atlanta, GA 30329

Murder
Parents of Murdered Children
100 E. 8th St., Suite B41
Cincinnati, OH 45202

Schizophrenia
Schizophrenics Anonymous
1209 California Rd.
Eastchester, NY 10709

Stroke
Stroke Clubs International
805 12th St.
Galveston, TX 77550

Sudden infant death
National Foundation for Sudden
Infant Death
330 N. Charles St.
Baltimore, MD 21201

National Sudden Infant Death
Syndrome Foundation
P. O. Box 2474
Landover Hills, MD 91784

Suicide
Heartbeat
2015 Devon St.
Colorado Springs, CO 80909

NOTES

Prologue

1. Metrick and Zelman, *Art From Ashes,* 7.
2. Lao-tzu, *Tao Te Ching,* 2.

Introduction

1. Imber-Black and Roberts, *Rituals in Families and Family Therapy,* 15.

Chapter 1. The Spectrum of Loss

1. Ruperti, *Cycles of Becoming,* 7.
2. Yalom, *Existential Psychotherapy,* 98.
3. Stewart, "Mental Hygiene and World Peace," *Mental Hygiene,* Vol. 38, No. 3.

Chapter 2. How Loss May Affect You

1. Klaber, "Fear and Loathing," *The Berkeley Monthly,* November 1993.
2. Hall, *The Moon and the Virgin,* 70, 71, 73.
3. Halifax, *Shaman,* 92.

Chapter 3. Healing through Grief or Mourning: The Journey toward Wholeness

1. Campbell, *Hero with a Thousand Faces,* 245.
2. *New American Bible,* 691.
3. Rando, *Grieving,* 11.

Chapter 4. Creative Expression and Ritual

1. Oddleifson, "The Case for the Arts," *In Context,* September 1990.
2. Stevens, *Poems of Wallace Stevens,* 30.
3. Erickson and Rossi, *Hypnotherapy,* 3.
4. Landy, "The Dramatic Bliss of Role Therapy," *The Arts in Psychotherapy,* Volume 18, 30.
5. Briggs, "The Magic of Masks," *Science Digest,* November 1985, 73.

Chapter 5. Creating a Ceremony

1. Mitchell, *Selected Poetry of Rainer Maria Rilke*, 73.
2. Lewis, *A Grief Observed*, 19, 20.

Chapter 6. Planning Your Ceremony

1. Bettleheim, *Uses of Enchantment*, 12.
2. Beck and Metrick, *Art of Ritual*, 73.

Chapter 7. Manifestation

1. Metrick and Zelman, *Art From Ashes*, 25.
2. Andrews, *Shakkai*, 35.
3. Jones, *Design for Death*, 246.
4. Sapolin, "The 'Pique' of Perfection," *Metropolitan Home*, July, 1990, 106.
5. Sargent, *Global Ritualism*, 78.

Chapter 8. Incorporation: Re-Writing the Story

1. May, *Cry for Myth*, 76, 77.
2. Ibid., 77.
3. Eliade, *Myth and Reality*, 140.
4. May, *Cry for Myth*, 50.

Chapter 10. Anniversaries

1. Vesper Hospice of the East Bay, San Leandro, CA.
2. Wang, *The Qabalistic Tarot*, 183.

Chapter 11. Death

1. Cohen, *The Circle of Life*, 223.
2. Ghia Gallery, San Francisco, CA.
3. AIDS Memorial Grove in Golden Gate Park, San Francisco, CA.
4. Imber-Black, Roberts, and Whiting, *Rituals in Families and Family Therapy*, 55.

REFERENCES AND FURTHER READING

Akhmatova, Anna. *Selected Poems.* Translated by Richard McKane. London, UK: Oxford University Press, 1969.

Andrews, Lynn V. *Shakkai.* New York: HarperCollins, 1992.

Arnold, Matthew. "Dover Beach." *The Portable Matthew Arnold.* New York: Viking Press, 1949.

Beck, Renee and Sydney Barbara Metrick. *The Art of Ritual.* Berkeley, CA: Celestial Arts, 1990.

Bettleheim, Bruno. *The Uses of Enchantment.* New York: Vintage Books, 1977.

Black Elk. *The Sacred Pipe.* Recorded and edited by Joseph Epes Brown. Norman, OK: University of Oklahoma Press, 1953.

Bolle, Kees W. *The Bhagavadita.* Berkeley, CA: University of California Press, 1979.

Briggs, John. "The Magic of Masks." *Science Digest,* November 1985.

Campbell, Joseph. *Primitive Mythology.* New York: Viking Penguin, 1987

Campbell, Joseph. *The Hero with a Thousand Faces.* New York: Princeton University Press, 1973.

Cavafy, C. P. *Collected Poems.* Translated by Edmund Keeley and Philip Sherrard. Edited by George Savidis. Princeton, NJ: Princeton University Press, 1975.

Cohen, David. *The Circle of Life.* San Francisco, CA: HarperSan Francisco, 1991.

Dershimer, Richard A. *Counseling the Bereaved.* New York: Pergamon Press, 1990.

Eliade, Mircea. *Myth and Reality.* New York: Harper and Row, 1963.

Eliot, T. S. *Four Quartets.* New York: Harcourt, Brace and World, 1943.

Emerson, Ralph Waldo. *Nature: Addresses and Lectures.* Boston, MA: Houghton Mifflin, 1876.

Erickson, Milton H. and Ernest L. Rossi. *Hypnotherapy: An Exploratory Casebook.* New York: Irvington Publishers, 1979.

Gadon, Elinor W. *The Once and Future Goddess.* San Francisco, CA: Harper and Row, 1989.

Gibran, Kahlil. *The Prophet.* New York: Alfred A. Knopf, 1923.

Halifax, Joan. *Shaman.* New York: Crossroad Publishing, 1982.

Hall, Nor. *The Moon and the Virgin.* New York: Harper and Row, 1980.

Highwater, Jamake. *Ritual at the Wind.* New York: Alfred Van der Marck Editions, 1984.

Houston, Jean. *The Search for the Beloved.* Los Angeles, CA: Jeremy Tarcher, 1987.

Imber-Black, E. and J. Roberts. *Rituals in Families and Family Therapy.* New York: W. W. Norton and Company, 1988.

Jones, Barbara. *Design for Death.* New York: Bobbs-Merrill Company, 1967.

Jung, C. G. *Psychological Types* , Volume 6. Translated by H. G. Barnes and revised by R.F.C. Hall. Princeton, NJ: Princeton University Press, 1971.

Klaber, Karen. "Fear and Loathing." *The Berkeley Monthly,* November 1993.

Kübler-Ross, Elizabeth. *Death: The Final Stage of Growth.* New York: Touchstone, 1975.

Landy, Robert J. "The Dramatic Basis of Role Therapy." *The Arts in Psychotherapy,* Volume 18, 1991.

Lao-tzu. *Tao Te Ching.* Translated by Stephen Mitchell. New York: Harper and Row, 1988.

Lehman, Arthur C. and James E. Myers. *Magic, Witchcraft and Religion.* Palo Alto, CA: Mayfield Publishing Company, 1985.

Levine, Stephen. *Healing into Life and Death.* Garden City, NY: Anchor/Doubleday, 1987.

Lewis, C. S. *A Grief Observed.* London: Faber & Faber, 1961.

May, Rollo. *The Cry for Myth.* New York: W. W. Norton and Company, 1991.

Metrick, Sydney and Diane Zelman. *Art From Ashes.* Oakland, CA: Marcus A. Foster Educational Institute, 1991.

Neihard, John G. *When the Tree Flowered.* New York: Simon and Schuster, Pocket Books, 1973.

New American Bible. Encino, CA: Benziger, 1970.

Oddleifson, Eric. "The Case for the Arts." *In Context,* September 1990.

Paigels, Elaine. *Gnostic Gospels.* New York: Vintage Books, 1979.

Plotinus. *The Essence of Plotinus.* Translated by Stephen MacKenna and compiled by Grace H. Turnbull. New York: Oxford University Press, 1948.

Ram Dass. *Grist for the Mill.* New York: Bantam Books, 1977.

Rando, Therese A. *Grieving: How to go on Living When Someone You Love Dies.* Lexington, MA: Lexington Books, 1988.

Regardie, Israel. *The Philosopher's Stone.* St. Paul, MN: Llewellyn Publications, 1970.

Rilke, Rainer Maria. "Requiem." The *Selected Poetry of Rainer Maria Rilke.* Edited and translated by Stephen Mitchell. New York: Random House, 1989.

Ruperti, Alexander. *Cycles of Becoming.* Davis, CA: CRCS Publications, 1978.

Sapolin, Donna. "The 'Pique' of Perfection." *Metropolitan Home,* July 1990.

Sargent, Denny. *Global Ritualism.* St. Paul, MN: Llewellyn Publications, 1994.

Shakespeare, William. *The Riverside Shakespeare.* Edited by G. Blakemore Evans. Boston: Houghton Mifflin, 1974.

Starhawk. *Spiral Dance,* New York: Harper and Row, 1979.

Stevens, Wallace. *Poems of Wallace Stevens.* New York: Vintage Books, 1947.

Stewart, Kilton. "Mental Hygiene and World Peace." *Mental Hygiene,* Vol. 38, No. 3.

The Upanishads. Translated by Alistair Shearer and Peter Russell. London, UK: Unwin Hyman, 1989.

Varene, Jean. *Yoga and the Hindu Tradition.* Chicago: University of Chicago Press, 1976.

Wang, Robert. *The Qabalistic Tarot.* York Beach, MI: Samuel Weiser, 1983

Yalom, Irvin. *Existential Psychotherapy.* New York: Basic Books, 1980

Other books you may enjoy from Celestial Arts:

The Art of Ritual
by Sydney Metrick and Renee Beck
A guide to creating and performing personalized rituals for growth and change. The authors discuss the importance of ritual in traditional cultures and show how to integrate it into modern life to celebrate births, achievements, special friendships, and other milestones.
$11.95 paper, 160 pages

I Do: A Guide to Creating Your Own Wedding Ceremony
by Sydney Metrick
Drawing on her experience designing and performing unique celebrations for a wide range of Bay Area couples, Ms. Metrick describes ceremonies for second or third marriages (often including one or both partner's children), interfaith, intercultural, and same sex marriages.
$11.95 paper, 160 pages

On Life After Death
by Elizabeth Kübler-Ross
Dr. Kübler-Ross's experiences, thoughts, and feelings on the afterlife fill these four inspirational essays. For the first time she gathers her vast research and comments on "Living and Dying," "There Is No Death," "Life, Death, and Life After Death," as well as the moving essay, "Death of a Parent."
$7.95 paper, 96 pages

Remember the Secret *by Elizabeth Kübler-Ross, illustrated by Heather Preston*
This beautiful story teaches about love, caring, and loss for children facing life-threatening illness or the loss of a loved one. A wonderful book for children to learn about the value of life as well as the reality of death and dying.
$9.95 paper, 32 pages

Forget Me Not: Caring and Coping with Your Aging Parents
by Alan P. Siegal and Robert Siegal
The average American woman will spend seventeen years raising her children and eighteen more years caring for her parents. This timely and supportive guide was developed to help those facing this situation. *Forget Me Not* is designed to assist in dealing with immediate medical situations, emotional fallout, and finding the resources needed to actually carry out plans.
$9.95 paper, 156 pages